Your Creative Edge

Chipo Shiloh Moyo

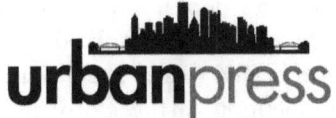

urbanpress

ENDORSEMENTS

"It takes courage to think, and to
think beyond where I am and what I don't have."

"Courage is truly the foundation upon which creativity is built. The
very fact that Chipo opens her book with this bold proclamation,
should prove that *Your Creative Edge* is a book worth reading. Being
a singer/songwriter, I understand the vulnerability and courage
it takes to put out original work for all to read or listen to, and
ultimately judge. I am proud of Chipo for taking this step of faith
to encourage the world to step into our God-given call to create."

Brian Nhira
Alum/Contestant NBC's Season 10 "The Voice"
Singer, Songwriter, Recording Artist

"In *Your Creative Edge*, Chipo has demystified the complexities,
pseudo thoughts and fallacies around the word Creative. Her depth
of Knowledge and passion is so inspiring and definitely convincing.
It is essential that one thinks outside of the box in the system
approach to this fast world today. Chipo expertise will force you to
have a paradigm shift in your mind and encourage you to conquer
yourself. If you desire to be effective, efficient and relevant in your
domain, this book is a must read!"

Prophetess and Pastor Grace Kapswara
International Conference Speaker
Jabula New Life Covenant Ministries
Harare, Zimbabwe

"Chipo Shiloh has a tender heart but a razor sharp spirit! She writes
Your Creative Edge with the necessary simplicity that is needed on
a subject that has been so confusing and opinionated. This book
will bring clarity to your gifts and passion while putting fresh
momentum inside of you to be on the frontlines of your call. Get
ready! This book is timely!"

Pastor Chris Estrada
Director, Youth For The Nations & Chris Estrada Ministries
Dallas, Texas

"Creativity. What is it? How does it "work?" What is our role in it?
What is God's role? These are questions asked by people everywhere
because there has never been a greater need to understand creativity
and express it as competition in the global marketplace expands
and opportunities for more entrepreneurs and creators present
themselves. In her first book, Chipo Moyo answers these questions

poses many others in *Your Creative Edge*. Her insight as a young African woman living in the United States adds an important, relevant voice to a growing body of material that addresses not only creativity but also women's issues and leadership."

Dr. John Stanko
President, Urban Press
President, PurposeQuest International

"Chipo is an irrepressible young lady. Her enthusiasm comes through every page. She will challenge you with her stories and her admonitions regarding the creative capacity we have by the Holy Spirit. You won't forget the force of her words."

Mike Massa
Founder, Convergence Ministries & Venture Heights Institute
Professor, Christ for the Nations Institute

"Our God is a God that inspires creativity and through this book he has revealed to Chipo how to take that creative edge and soar like an eagle. This page-turner reminds me of a time I would enjoy Chipo's dedication to art as she would make birthday cards that had a prophetic story. She would also teach our children in the Children's Church how to be creative and she would light up our offices with her inventiveness. Its a must read for every woman! I believe that anyone who reads this book will be inspired to take up the creativity that God has planted in them and affect generations to come."

Pastor Prisca Maphiwa
Lead Pastor, Celebration Church Kenya
Logos University, Jacksonville, FL USA

"It is with honor I have been asked to endorse this book. I have watched Chipo grow in many areas of her life over the years. She is certainly a creative and prayerful woman with an incredible prophetic gifting and undeniable passion for the things of God. *Your Creative Edge* is a necessary book every woman needs to get their hands on. I believe it is a timely and prophetic word for our generation and a call to all women to seek out and find or embrace their creative mandate from God. Once you pick this book up you won't want to put it down. Every lady of purpose needs to discover their creative edge!"

Pastor Fungayi Spencer-Mumme
Founder and President, Ladies of Purpose Intl. Ministries
Senior Pastor, Forward in Faith Church, Boston, MA USA

For Worldwide Distribution
Printed in the U.S.A.

Urban Press
P.O. Box 8881
Pittsburgh, PA 15221-0881 USA
412.646.2780
www.urbanpress.us

Thank You, Lord, for the privilege and
honor You have given me to create.

CONTENTS

INTRODUCTION

If you hate creativity, you may go a little nuts in this book. And if confessions are allowed . . . I honestly had no clue what I was going to say about creativity when I started writing this book. I think what caught me a little off guard was how something that is so easy for me to do, was so hard for me to write about. However, if you have managed to read this far, here goes . . .

Creativity is my God-given birthright. This book was birthed out of a personal conviction I had. The conviction of ideas that I have contained in the seams of my life, that need to burst out and be seen. It is a huge thing to imagine that we came from a Creator Who created all things and in Whom all things are held together.

If there were any reservations about God being creative and having a delightful sense of humor, I would suggest you check on Elijah's story, who was starving and was fed by a bird—but later, he took off to Heaven and disappeared in some rather interesting aerodynamics (without a boarding pass). Some witnessed burning bushes and parting Red Seas. Quail fell down like rain; then there was manna, strange weather, and rainbows. Unique praise battle strategies, instant leprosy, talking donkeys, a sling-shot and a shepherd boy conquering a giant, money in a fish's mouth, water turning to wine, a star used as a billboard to broadcast the birth of Jesus, or Jonah who had to go on a time-out for disobedience in the belly of a whale. Then there was Lot's wife, who experienced a rather salty punishment for her disobedience. God's creative power is the thread that holds everything together and adds color to not only the lives of many characters in the Bible, but to my life and yours as well.

I realized I could not exhale greatness when I continue to inhale failure. It takes courage to think, and to think beyond where I am and what I don't have. I decided that I would have the courage today, to believe in my own ideas, and walk in their manifestation and fulfillment. The thought "What if," what if I did try—became louder than what would go wrong if I tried.

The other day I was watching my nephews; they are twins who just turned one. They cannot walk yet, but they can stand with the support of a table or other object. I was challenged by something one of them did. The older one Shane is very quiet, collected and loves to be left alone to play on his terms. He is not very demanding and an easygoing baby who can do without my endless hugs and kisses. His younger brother Shawn on the other hand thrives on hugs and kisses. He loves to be the center of attention and if ignored he will throw a tantrum.

Shawn disappeared in his parents' two-story house the other day, as he frequently does, and several minutes later his mother heard giggling coming from the ceiling. She looked up and there was Shawn, sitting upstairs by the balcony, waving at everyone in the living room downstairs. He had climbed up the long set of winding stairs, mind you, he cannot walk yet. His mother calmly bolted up the stairs to get him before he could figure out how to come back down. His curiosity is a little dangerous at times, but he is showing signs that he will start walking much sooner than Shane.

If you could tour their home, it is very easy to see where Shawn has left the scene of the crime—broken cupboard handles, laptops missing keys, broken phone screens, chewed remote controls, broken toys, and stray diapers. He is an active explorer, and there isn't a room downstairs he has not been in. His brother Shane plays it safe, staying in the same room, but Shawn is all over the place.

Some of us are like Shane. We play it safe and stay in the places we are most comfortable, but comfort is an enemy to growth. However, if we are like Shawn, curious with a "the earth is the Lord's and fullness thereof" attitude and ready for every creative adventure, we will see every moment as an opportunity to look, listen and learn.

My life is not picture perfect, but in writing this book I wanted to make a commitment to you, to share the best of what I have learned, what I am learning and what I am believing God for. If anything, I want you to read this book, and by the time you put it down, you can't wait to go do that thing you have been procrastinating about or given up on. May reading this book motivate you to leave the comfort of your past and the limitations of your present situation to start living with your future in mind. Expect to be inspired, provoked, laugh, experience a streak of discomfort, and to encounter my devotion and invitation to explore getting out and over yourself and express the meaningful creative life God created you to have.

PART 1
GOD'S IMAGE

CHAPTER ONE
LET US MAKE MAN IN OUR IMAGE AND LIKENESS

"For we are His workmanship,
created in Christ Jesus for good works,
which God prepared beforehand
that we should walk in them"
(Ephesians 2:10).

It is hard to comprehend that we have the privilege of living in a world, teeming with so much creativity. Sometimes I have to pinch myself because I am enamored by how incredible and ingenious God is. It is through His manifold wisdom that we experience one of nature's most feared predators, capable of killing animals twice its size, the biggest and fiercest cat, the Tiger. Out of God's wisdom, we see the tasteful proportions and perfections of spots or stripes sported by leopards, jaguars, cheetahs and zebras. The bioluminescent organs (glow in the dark effect) in a Jellyfish, the epic proportions and regenerative qualities of the baobab tree, the intricacy and intelligence in the human central nervous system, the blanket of galaxies that seem to have no end and the outrageous, graceful and clumsy necks of tropical lush pink and orange flamingos, herons, camels and spotted giraffes.

God's stuff always blows me away; it is no wonder His Word says our wisdom is mere foolishness to God. I am in awe when I try to imagine that God spoke all creatures, oceans and land masses into existence and they happened; then He said, "Let Us make man in our image and likeness." I have often wondered what it meant to be created in both His "image" and "likeness," and why He didn't just say the one word. I always felt like there was an added hidden bonus there that God threw in and I was unaware of. And that led me on a bunny trail of all sorts of research, so here goes . . .

The image speaks of His rulership and authority, and the likeness applies to His relational qualities. The "image" refers to being created with ruling and kingly qualities and the "likeness" involves the relationship of sonship that we have with God. Our God-given task in creation is to carry out the task of a king, and relate to God as sons. It is fascinating to imagine the magnitude of creative power, the vocational and instrumental qualities we possess, and even more so to our responsibility as we mirror God in His creativity, love, generosity, authority, dominion, and acceptance. I find myself pondering Isaiah 46:20,

"Declaring the end from the beginning
and from ancient times things that are not yet done,
saying 'My counsel shall stand,
And I will do all my pleasure.'"

How amazing it is to imagine that God is not confined by time or history; He fulfills every necessary step to His purpose.

A Strategic Creator

A level of responsibility came with the privilege, but our sense of responsibility was challenged and tested by the Fall. The Fall did not remove the image God put on us, but it certainly damaged our ability to relate to God, to people and to the created order of all things. As a result, we don't fully manifest what the image of God should look like because we have been injured by sin. But thankfully, the image of God is still imprinted on us; He never changed, but through sin we did.

Genesis 9:6 tells us: "Whoever sheds man's blood. By man his blood shall be shed; for in the image of God He made man." Cain sinned against God and murdered Abel, but the image of God still remained. The gifts of God are without repentance, but we have been given the responsibility to steward those gifts.

Creative Order

God does everything He does in an orderly fashion. He created our bodies with systems that are orderly and to serve a specific function. The Human body has various systems, the circulatory system, digestive system, endocrine system, reproductive system, respiratory system, excretion system, nervous systems, immune system, skeletal system and muscle system. The human body has profound engineering that outshines everything else God made. God's structural nature is seen in the beginning in Genesis through God's creative expressions. "God said" was a structural announcement, "Let there be" was a creative decree, "And it was so" marked a point of accomplishment in what God was doing, "… the earth brought forth" is descriptive of God's accomplishments in creation, and then "God blessed" marking a point of blessing in what God had done. Then, "It was good" speaks of His Divine evaluation of what manifested when God spoke.

Words are not enough to express or describe what God has created. It is a lot to take in when you understand how heavy the earth is, and yet, it hangs quite securely in the universe like a giant Christmas tree ornament, floating in the midst of God's purpose, glory and design in space according to Job 26:7. The Universe obeys God's ordinances for Heaven and earth. According to Jeremiah 33:25, there are mathematics that God has set in place by His design. The laws of physics, chemistry and biology operate on God's clock and for His purposes—everything God does is precise. Everything obeys God's strict ordinances concerning times and seasons—the sun, moon and stars appear at their proper time. I am intrigued by God's creative consistency and His artful precision.

A Rhythmic Creator

Everything God does has a rhythm. Rhythm governs every second of our lives. Even our lives are lived with a rhythm that we are either conscious of or completely unaware of. Rhythm in the ticking of a clock; it is in every breath we take, in the sound of a heartbeat, the clapping of hands, the beating of birds' wings, or the sound of train wheels on a track. There is even a rhythm to the thinking patterns we have, languages we speak, the footsteps we take, and even the belt on the airport baggage carousel has a series of clacking sounds.

There is some objective component to rhythm, and it is mostly composed of feeling. Some rhythms come from revelations we have about the Word of God, our experiences and things we learn from family. When I go through challenging experiences that shift my focus, I notice I end up losing my rhythm. Sometimes, it is hard to get back into it. A problem sometimes arises from emotions, impatience and impulsiveness, which can easily overshadow my rhythm. I know there are times I have lost my rhythm the moment I decided to force things to go in a direction God did not say they should go.

Pastor Mark Chironna puts it so well, "The flow of destiny has a rhythm to it, a choreography." (Chironna, Mark. 2015). There are two men who walked in rhythm with God, Enoch and Noah. They walked in rhythm with God because they agreed with God. Rhythm is not just a response from the outside (pace), but it is a response that flows out of the very core of who we are. Timing is also connected to rhythm. In music, rhythm is the placement of sounds in time. I am reminded of the way my metronome beats, and it helps train me to maintain a good tempo. It helps to regulate and measure my playing ability. The Holy Spirit is like the metronome that helps me walk in rhythm with God.

God has established the universe and everything is in its rightful place. God did not create anything by accident; everything He made serves a purpose. The gifts and talents He has given all serve a purpose; no gift is without significance, and everything God gives has a purpose attached to it. It is important to search for the purpose even in my own creative abilities, because this adds a greater perspective to the creative process.

A Divine Tapestry of Rhythm

Nature is infinitely rich in structure. Bees produce stellar honey without having a recipe, and they certainly have a knack for geometry. Bees have the instinct to produce symmetry in a beehive that humans can only reproduce with a compass and a ruler. One of the most intriguing things in Creation is the consistency of pattern and rhythm. Without having any instructions, a blueprint or guidance, grains, molecules, fluids, particles and tissues are able to arrange themselves into geometrical patterns. God's creation is sheer genius, and thinking about all of this gives me Goosebumps!

There is symmetry everywhere around us. There is symmetry in human lungs, facial structures, and peacock feathers, cactuses, on animals, even in water droplets. Ferns have a pattern, leaves; even lightning follows a path step by step as it moves toward the ground. Waterfalls flow in a pattern as they cascade over irregular jagged rocks pulled by gravity culminating in a repeated pattern of water gushing against a scenic background. The regular cycles of days, seasons and life have a rhythm and pattern. The crescent shaped Namibian sand dunes, spider webs hidden in the Amazon jungle, spirals of pinecone scales in North America, the ripples in the Indian Ocean created by the wind all carry a distinct rhythm and pattern.

It's amazing to see how mathematical God is, the symmetry, tessellations, mirror reflections, regularity, rotational and radial symmetry in water drops splashing in a puddle of water. The spots and stripes on leopards, ladybugs, zebras and the royal angelfish all carry a symmetry and regularity that surpasses our understanding. The never-ending fractals and spirals in trees, rivers, mountains, meandering rivers, clouds, and the horns of sheep. Hurricanes also manifest in spirals, galaxies and seashells; in fact the entire galaxy looks like a giant seashell! The Fibonacci patterns in pineapples, pinecones, and flower petals of flowers like lilies and sunflowers. I was not a fan of math in school, but there is so much geometry and synthesis in nature it is mind-blowing to see just how rhythmic and mathematical God is.

Our Creative Authority

We were created to subdue, and subdue means to master, impose, bring order and develop, to put our imprint on creation in a positive way. God has not called us to violate and rape our environment, but to subdue and to rule. God's creativity operates with words, a clue that whatever we say can change everything about our world. God's creative word power carries immeasurable significance that created dimensions, systems, rank, and relationships. We see throughout the Bible undeniable evidence of the power of a spoken word. Jesus performed miracles, signs and wonders with words; our highest call to worship has paved the way for expression of God's love through sound and words. Kingdoms are established and removed by words, and the preaching and teaching of the Word changes our lives. We also have been given permission to create with our words.

CHAPTER TWO
IMAGO DEI

"And Jesus said to them,
'Render to Caesar the things that are Caesar's
and to God the things that are God's ...'"
(Mark 12:17).

Creativity matters to God. God created more than seven billion images of Himself and put them on this earth. I think that is pretty impressive! And part of His plan was for those seven billion images to reflect His glory. God knew when He said He had created us in His image, we would later be confronted with images that would challenge what He said. When we come to know the Lord, we bring a lifetime of experiences and behaviors that affect how we perceive that moment of salvation. We all experience the moment God touches our lives, but we all walk away with a unique interpretation of it.

Sometimes some of us get caught up in wanting other peoples' stories, or our stories to be like those of others and end up missing the story that God has already written for us. Even children, as babies, will look at their mother's face for clues to who they are and often look for mom's approval (International, Inc. Advanced Solutions). Through adulthood, our fallen man is predisposed to search for who it is in the things around us. William Swann, a psychology professor from University of Texas at Austin says, "People rely on others' impressions to nurture their view about themselves." God knew we would look at other things for our identities, so in the beginning, He made sure we knew we were His by letting us know we were created in His image.

A Chaotic Environment

Creativity is birthed in the womb of chaos, and God created order out of chaos. The Bible says that, "In the beginning God created the heavens and the earth. The earth was formless and void, and darkness was over the surface of the deep, and the Spirit of God was moving over the surface of the waters. Then God said, 'Let there be light;' and there was light." Even the darkest, void and desolate places of our lives are perfect environments for a move of God.

God's creation and its variety reminds me that there is definitely something special God had in mind. God has created all of us with some pretty outrageous individuality. The varieties of birds, plants and mammals for example are a reminder to me that there are several ways to express the same thing and get the job done. The same applies to creative ideas—every idea always serves a unique function and carries a unique expression and purpose. When God does something it is not just functional but beautiful as well. What God can do is defying all imagination. The essence of God is variety, and we possess the same sense of variety in our creative mandate.

His Imago Dei

In Genesis 1:27, Imago Dei is a theological term meaning the image of God, and it should manifest in every part of our lives. His Image is an awareness of qualities God has put in our lives. It is a deposit that He has made. I often try to imagine the scene where God breathed life into Adam in the Book of Genesis. I wonder if God gently or forcefully breathed into Adam's nostrils, and what God breathed into him. God breathed His mind, His presence, His essence, His thoughts, His creative prowess, His forceful nature, His dominion. I wonder what exactly God gave me when He gave me life?

God's creativity is not exhaustible, and neither is ours. He has given us the ability to discover new things or find new things in existing things. I think of a drawing—in art the skill of drawing is not so much in the technicalities of drawing, but also about "seeing skill." When you draw, you don't just see a bowl of fruit, but you see light, shadows, negative space, and relations of the whole. I see the Image of God in a similar light. His image is not so much a physical appearance as it is in my characteristics and nature—the things about me that I cannot read at face value. The Image of God can refer not to the things He has hidden from me, but the things He has hidden for me.

It is scary to imagine that my life may be loaded with potential that I may be completely unaware of. I often wonder, "Lord, what is it about me that you have put on the inside of me that I am choosing not to see?" The enemy did not start studying my life the moment I became a Christian; he has been deceiving and studying my heritage for more than 4,000 years; his deception knows my history, my heritage, my lineage, my weaknesses and the prevalent patterns in my bloodline. This is more than enough reason for me to seek and find what God has hidden on the inside of me.

His case studies began with Adam, and have never stopped since. The enemy is quick to present partial or incomplete truth; his deception has a strategy he uses to remind me of how sinful I am, but he leaves out the part about how God's grace is not for perfect people. I thank God that "He remembers that we are dust" (Psalm 103:13, 14).

Image Perception

Perception plays a huge part in how and what I decide to do with my life and the reality I experience. Perception is also the filter I see and evaluate through. A poor perception of creative ability will always default to limitations, mistakes, and a choice to believe the lies and accusations of the enemy.

Our perceptions are often influenced by our thoughts and our postures. Our bodies can change our minds, and our minds can change our behavior, which can change our outcomes (Cuddy, 2012). Have you ever been in one of those trying seasons? Sometimes, we get so overwhelmed by the circumstances during those seasons. The reality of it is so real that we often feel imprisoned by the circumstance, being permanently stuck. I had a recent 'aha' moment after going through a series of trials in my life. The single freedom I had in that moment was that the enemy could not take away my perception and how I chose to respond. In that moment I imagined myself in a better place, overcoming. When I look back at this, in that moment, I realized, "Wait a minute, I got this!" Perception is more powerful than what we think; it can influence behavior and the creative reality we will live in.

God had a purpose in creating me in His image, and it is through my perception of His image that I am able to have confidence to "draw near to the throne of grace, that I may receive mercy and find grace to help in time of need" (Hebrews 4:16). The image I bear is a gift from Christ; it is not achieved or earned; it is given by grace. I see God revealed in the Word. When God spoke, His spoken Word released something into my life that spoke of my rank, my purpose, my privilege and my potential.

Inspired by God

We take for granted more often than we think; that most if not all of the inspiration we get to create comes from what God has already created. God's creation is the source of inspiration for everything we do. God is the origin of creativity. Landscape photographers take pictures of the perfectly chiseled rocks and mountains God designed. Fine Artists and Fashion designers are inspired by the rich pigments in flowers, leaves and minerals, and the entire backdrop of creation, which is constantly teeming with color and texture.

CHAPTER THREE
THE HOLY SPIRIT

"But God has revealed them to us through His Spirit.
For the Spirit searches all things, yes,
the deep things of God.
For what man knows the things of a man
except the spirit of the man which is in him?
Even so no one knows the things of God except the Spirit of God.
Now we have received, not the spirit of the world,
but the Spirit who is from God,
that we might know the things that have been freely
given to us by God"
(1 Corinthians 2:10).

The word is so full of God's creative presence. His creative thread connects and weaves together song, poetry, biography, letters, love stories, narratives, parables, proverbs and prophecy. The creative consistency of scripture would not be possible without a unifying person of God, the Holy Spirit. Creativity is about relationship, and its essence comes out of a relationship with God. Artists were the first people to be filled with Holy Spirit. The Spirit came on Zechariah and Azariah, but Bezalel was filled with the Holy Spirit in Exodus 31:1-5. The arts must be important to God.

"Then the LORD spoke to Moses, saying:
'See, I have called by name Bezalel the son of Uri,
the son of Hur, of the tribe of Judah.
And I have filled him with the Spirit of God,
in wisdom, in understanding, in knowledge,

and in all *manner of* workmanship, to design artistic works,
to work in gold, in silver, in bronze,
in cutting jewels for setting,
in carving wood, and to work
in all *manner of* workmanship.'"

God wanted His tabernacle to be a place of creative expression. This spoke to me in volumes of how important creative expression is in the Church. God filled Bezalel with His Spirit, to accomplish His work. May God fill you and me with His Spirit to accomplish the task He lays before us. I learned three things from the story about Bezalel. First, God chooses whom He will give the gifts to, and God gave Bezalel the gift He wanted him to have. Second, the Spirit of God is involved in God's creative acts, and He brought about the creation of all things in the Book of Genesis. Third, God's gifts serve a purpose.

The Tabernacle and the Golden Calf

I could not help but think of the difference between the Tabernacle and the golden calf. I was reading this passage of scripture the other day and was asking the Holy Spirit why the golden calf angered God so much. As I read about it in Exodus 26-28, I saw that the Tabernacle was requested by God. Moses was instructed by God to take offerings for it of gold, silver and bronze, and everyone was to give wholeheartedly. There was also a specific model of how God wanted it to look with intricate details of measurements, colors, materials, etc. There were detailed descriptions God gave Moses of dedication procedures, anointing oil, the priestly garments and several other specifics. God was calling the Israelites to be "Holy as He is Holy." The Tabernacle was so special because it was designed to mirror exactly what God said.

Bezalel was also called by God to be a craftsman— everything was orderly, complete and ordained by God. The Tabernacle was a reflection of God's Divine leading. And it was an external assurance of His tangible presence working in every part of the Israelites lives.

The golden calf on the other hand was also created from offerings of gold, but it was created without a divine command from God. It was not created out of obedience but out of fear and the flesh. Unlike Bezalel, Aaron was not called to be a craftsman by God; he was self-appointed. The whole incident was chaotic and a reflection of ignorance and weakness. It was a reflection of very hasty and haphazard leadership, simply driven by compulsion without any reverence for God. It was essentially an external evidence to satisfy an inner insecurity the Israelites had from the days of bondage in Egypt.

The Tabernacle had all those intricate details because God wanted us to know that His presence was perfect, and that true beauty and orderliness was found in His presence. Reading this and then hearing from God scared me a little because it made me wonder what things in my life was I doing or making that were golden calves? It made me think about the condition of my heart, my motives, and my attitude toward the gifts God has given me. Honestly, I thought about my weaknesses, and what kind of "Egyptian baggage" I was allowing to creep into my life. What was I doing with my life that was a reflection of ignorance, flesh and weakness?

Time and Chance

We all are given an opportunity to birth things and to create things. Some have chosen a personal relationship with God, with Jesus and with the Holy Spirit, and others have rejected Him. I have often wondered why some of the most innovative ideas and creative inventions were created by those who were not Christians. Then the Lord took me to the verse in Ecclesiastes 9:11 which says,

> *"I returned and saw under the sun that-*
> *The race is not to the swift,*
> *Nor the battle to the strong,*

Nor bread to the wise,
Nor riches to men of understanding,
Nor favor to men of skill;
But time and chance happen to them all."

We all have been given time and chance. God's sun shines on the just and the unjust. Creativity can either work for us or against us; it is a dangerous and wonderful thing that is not necessarily OR directly compatible with our faith. Our faith is what unites us and that sense of unity or the culture may be what causes us to share the same system of meaning about certain things. Creativity involves breaking the mold and seeing things in a way they have never been seen before.

If we study the lives of those who have made any lasting impact or contribution to creativity, they had to be trailblazers and start something that had not been done, or refine something that was already there. There is no reason why creative people cannot be believers or unbelievers; time and chance has been given to us all.

In the life of a believer, the Holy Spirit has a special part to play. He is the oil that gives us Divine enablement. The Holy Spirit was brooding over the waters, and then God said, "Let there be light." Would light have manifested if the Holy Spirit had not brooded over the waters? I think ideas are like eggs and the Holy Spirit is like the eagle that broods over them to incubate and protect them, and cause them to hatch. During creation He was there brooding over us, and when we have an idea or are creating, He brings to our remembrance the things God has already freely given to us.

The Holy Spirit helps us connect with God and understand the things God has so freely given us. He teaches us to discern the voice of God, as God's voice will often lead us to places we can never get to on our own. In order to discover the purpose of our creative endowment, it is necessary to be deeply connected to God, to connect with the purpose of our craft.

The Tempo of our Call

What God has to say is always more important than what I already know and what I am going through. I love how the Lord reminds us that, "Apart from Him, we cannot do anything" (John 15:5). I was reading in 1 John 2:27, "As for you, the anointing which you received from Him abides in you, and you have no need for anyone to teach you; but as His anointing teaches you about all things, and is true and is not a lie, and just as it has taught you, you abide in Him."

The Anointing and Outpouring of the Holy Spirit teaches us all things, the things God has freely given to us. The Holy Spirit is important to everything; He knows what we are supposed to do with the things God has given us. He garnishes the Heavens (Job 26:13), He was brooding over the waters during creation (Genesis 1:2), He renews the earth (Psalm 104:30), He sustains our lives everyday (Psalm 104:109). His work is never without results, as He brings order out of chaos, life (Job 33:4), beauty, restoration and renewal (Psalm 104:30.)

I mentioned briefly in an earlier chapter that the Holy Spirit is like the metronome that helps us keeps the right tempo for our lives. As a musician, I practice a lot with my metronome; it helps me keep in time when I am working on a piece of music. The Holy Spirit is like the metronome in other ways. He helps me develop my inner sense of rhythm for the things of God. He helps me keep in time with the music of my life, so when 'kairos' opportunities present themselves, I am ready. The Holy Spirit also helps by giving me markings for where God (my Composer) wants to communicate the tempo of my calling.

Creativity requires risk, for there is the possibility of failure and rejection, and the Holy Spirit gives all of us that boldness to take risks, regardless of the opposition, rejection, or suffering we may endure. He is the One Who enables us to stand in the authority of who we were created to be and not stagger at the promises of God (Romans 4:20-25).

Creativity involves selflessness. When we create, we give, and not for personal gain. The Holy Spirit through His indwelling can help us remember that we are trees that are called to bear fruit, and that as a tree, you don't eat your own fruit, but others around you benefit from your fruit. He helps keep things in God's perspective.

It takes a measure of faith to create, especially when you have nothing to work with. God releases ideas, without a full report and map on how everything is going to pan out, but as God releases that idea (the egg), the Holy Spirit (eagle) broods over what God said, and helps us to visualize the possibilities of that idea. We often shortchange ourselves when we see where we are, what we don't have, what others did to us, or what others think of us. However, He sees who we could be. He reveals and releases our potential, lays our capabilities before us, and helps us pursue our possibilities.

The Holy Spirit can change our perspective of ourselves and of God. He often does this by stripping away the things we depend on that will compete with God's sovereignty and place in our lives. He causes us to be empowered by God and not by our resources or the resources of others.

A Personal Encounter with the Holy Spirit

Several years ago, I had a series of encounters with the Lord. I will share one particular encounter, where I had a dream. I had this very deep desire to learn how to draw. It was a desire that would not go away. Growing up I could draw, but it was very average. In high school, I was always at the bottom of my art class, but after I came to know Christ, something happened to me. You know when something is hidden so deeply within your heart that you can't erase it? I don't think I ever verbally asked God to give me the gift, but there was a part of me that knew He knew how I felt, and that He had heard my heart.

It was through this that I understood what it meant to

be given the desires of my heart by the Lord. I had a dream one night where there was something like an earthquake in my bedroom. Suddenly, I was sitting on my bed in my room, and the ceiling above me started to peel open like a giant can. I saw this piercing, bright gold light. I remember the presence of God was so thick I could almost taste it, and as soon as the light touched me, I saw many different colors of pencil crayons suddenly fall from Heaven—it was a thunderstorm of crayons. I have never seen that many crayons at the same time, and they fell on me so quickly. As soon as they touched me, I screamed. The crayons kept falling, like lightning and rain, and then I woke up and gasped. I actually sat up in my bed from the dream because I was so shocked by what had just happened.

I pondered over the dream for days. One day, when I was in church in a service, I felt this fire brush against me as if someone had walked in front of me and sat down. The Holy Spirit whispered in my ear and I started to cry. He said, "Those were not crayons that I gave you, but creative gifts."

PART 2
MY
IMAGE

CHAPTER FOUR
CREATED OUT OF LOVE AND TO EXPRESS LOVE

"We love Him because He first loved us"
(1 John 4:19).

Love is powerful because it connects us with each other and with God. God created us to love and then gave us the capacity to operate out of His multi-dimensional love. We are gifted with different expressions of love that we can give and receive all at the same time. There is the love between a man and a woman, the love a father has for a son, the love between a mother and daughter, the love and loyalty that two brothers share, and the love and friendship between sisters, the love for those who have been rejected and forsaken by others, the love we have for people we don't know, the love for the Body of Christ and the love for those who are lost and are in need of Jesus Christ. Children were meant to come out of the consummation of love and be nurtured in a loving relationship between a man and woman.

Statistics for the number of people who feel unloved is shocking, even in the Church. The love of God has been evicted from the minds and the hearts of people. It is impossible to walk in love in a culture that tells us to only love ourselves or to love only those who do good things to us. I have often missed the point of God's love because I was guilty of partially giving my attention to God and hardly to the people He created for me to love.

Humanity did not come out of need or deficiency, but out of God's glory and His love. Our physical appearances, emotional and physical makeup, our history, gifts and the way we relate to others are different from one person to the next. Our many differences speak of God's love for us, that the Creator loved us all enough to put something special and different in each one of us.

I love how His actions flow from His very nature, which is His love. I was fashioned by love and because of Love. I know He loved me because:

1. He fashioned a world I could benefit from.
2. He created a theatre where His redemptive plan would manifest.
3. He created a living being and put His Spirit inside of Him.
4. It is seen in the "very good" comments He made in the Book of Genesis.
5. He made me out of the essence of Who He is … Love.

Let us Keep Creating

One thing about the love of God is that it is consistent. I am often quick to give up on an idea because I think it's average or others say it's a waste of time, but sometimes the secret is to keep working and digging deeper until all the average ideas are out of the way and the right idea shows up. It's also like building a bridge—some ideas are part of the process of building the bridge that will get you across to the other side.

There are times I create things that just don't work, or half work or leave me wondering why I even created it in the first place. But no matter what I have to tell myself to never ever stop because there are things within me and all of us that are too important NOT to try.

In God's love and creative power, we see His character, and His commitment. Creating, whether you are creating with sound, with words, with color, with fabrics, with chemicals, with numbers, with positive and negative space, with people, etc., requires consistency.

I was inspired by renowned author, Maya Angelou, who had a writing schedule. She rented a room in a hotel where she went to write. She loved to write and wrote consistently from 6 a.m.–2 p.m., and edited her work at home. I am sure there are things she wrote that remain unpublished, but what mattered is that she never gave up on creating and sharpening her craft.

Consistency requires a level of passion, conviction and discipline. The hardest thing for me has been creating, even when I felt like I was moving against the tide and not with it.

Love is sacrificial and requires an investment. Creating the things I love requires an investment. God gave me access to all of His resources and His love when He created the universe. God did not create anything that would bring Him loss or debt, but He created out of the abundance of His love, and He sees the return on His investment every day because all of creation worships Him. Creativity that flows from a place of revelation of the love of God widens and deepens my worship experiences. We are called to create through the lens of love, with our hearts, our minds, our strength and our souls. An important principle is to value the intimacy and privilege of partnering with God in every creative endeavor. Our creative abilities are knitted, intertwined and connected to God as our Source of love.

I am challenging myself to lovingly invest more in my craft. Let's face it. The feel-good activities that have no true value are easier to do, but these often have no positive long-term returns. The problem often stems from the perspective I have of myself and of what creativity is. The hardest person to love is often myself. If creativity flows out of love, but if I have an unhealthy attitude toward my capabilities and myself, it can be detrimental to my creative process. Low self-image for many years affected many things about myself. I often would be around people who I had just met who thought I were creative, but I often wondered what they were seeing that I failed to see. God has healed me from that, but it has been a process. Because I did not love myself, I had a damaged mental outlook that was playing a very negative part in what I expressed.

Trusting that what I created was valuable could not come from other people's evaluations, but from knowing my personal worth in Christ. The way I saw myself was emanating from my belief system. And often what held me back were my beliefs about myself. It is important to allow God to rewrite your belief system if it is damaged by life's experiences; otherwise, you will keep getting results in life that you don't want.

A Lesson from a Loving Leader

There is a powerful example of a leader who was so selfless and loved his country. Confinement in a prison did not confine his vision or his love for his nation. At times, when he felt very low, he cited the poem: (Henley William E., 1900):

"I am the master of my fate;
I am the captain of my soul."

The man I am talking about is the first black and former President of South Africa, Nelson Mandela. He was confined to an 8 x 7 foot prison, was ill-treated and isolated for 27 years. His prison wardens did not allow him to even attend his mother or brother's funeral when they passed. President Mandela had many opportunities to be bitter, angry and seek revenge for all those years he was mistreated, but he forgave, trusting that forgiveness for him was a way to build a bridge of reconciliation, instead of burning that bridge.

President Mandela created peace from sports, no matter how badly he was treated. It was an act of love that led him to embrace the Springboks as a way transcending racial boundaries in South Africa. The Springboks represented segregation and racism, but he saw them as a symbol for reconciliation and hope. When the Springboks won the 1995 Rugby world cup, Nelson Mandela was cited, saying by Piers Edwards in a CNN article (Friday 6 December 2013), "Sport has the power to change the world," and "It has the power to inspire."

Madiba, as he was affectionately known, went out on the field before a crowd of 65,000 people in the stadium on the day of the game. An audience that was 95 percent white, and he wore a green Springbok jersey, the old symbol of oppression. There was a moment of jaw dropping disbelief, but suddenly the crowd started to chant his name "Nelson, Nelson, Nelson!" Nelson Mandela knew the rugby jersey was a symbol of oppression, but he also knew it was also a symbol of something the Springbok supporters loved. He knew that to win his enemy over the capacity to love and to forgive was more powerful than oppression. He once stated that, "People learn to hate, but if they can learn to hate, they can also be taught to love." I think he was a creative leader because he understood how powerful love was, and through his actions, he challenged the moral compass and mindset of his oppressors.

Love the Creative Process

The creative process is one that is full of surprises! It requires much courage and discipline to embrace it. I think it is often difficult to love the process when you don't understand it or you don't have room for it. Learning to make space for new ideas, sounds, people, experiences, and insights helps to break off old ways of thinking. I have often gotten caught up in reaching a particular place of accomplishment and neglected that the process was just as important. Starting with questions is just as important as finding answers. It is important to look ahead even when you are in the midst of an accomplishment, so your next idea can "ride the tail" of the current wave of success. Loving your craft comes from knowing your Creator and what you value. Our love for the Lord is what should bring our ideas to a place where they touch the people who will experience them. Be deeply connected to God and you will be deeply connect to your craft, which will connect others to God.

> **"Love creates a communion with life.**
> **Love expands us, connects us,**
> **sweetens us, enables us."**
> **– Jack Kornfield**

CHAPTER FIVE
A PERSONAL CREATIVE EXPERIENCE

"For we are His workmanship,
created in Christ for good works,
which God prepared beforehand,
that we should walk in them"
(Ephesians 2:10).

Phew...okay so this is officially the chapter I get to expose a few of my "creative childhood shenanigans". My life like yours is filled with stories of childhood creative mischief. My parents often did not know what to do with my brother and I. As I sit and reflect, I feel a sense of remorse for what I put my poor parents through; mom and dad if you are reading this, I apologize again for all for the foolish things I did as a child . . . here goes . . .

Growing up, we spent many of our days either on timeout, spanked or deprived of our TV privileges for our "frequent creative outbursts." My brother and I are the product of a jazz musician/engineer/tech enthusiast and a fashion designer/artist/writer. If you don't mind, I will share a few fond memories; during one school holiday, we must have been 9 and 5 years old, while mom and dad were at work, we decided we would open a shopping mall in my brother's bedroom, we took everything out of my brother's room including the curtains, bed, clothing, toys etc. Our caregiver was conveniently doing laundry all day outside.

This was one of our "big ideas" as two little African children with nothing constructive to do. After clearing our "mall" space, we carefully inspected the entire house for potential products to display. Our first stop was our father's music studio, where we helped ourselves with no restraint, to dad's vinyl records, videotapes, engineering tools and musical instruments. The next stop was their bedroom where we grabbed clothing; jewelry, shoes and anything small enough to carry that belonged to mom. With a sense of pride and purpose, we carefully lined the shelves in my brother's room with the items we had "borrowed," and I found an empty cardboard box we turned into a cash register and some plastic grocery bags to bag items.

We found some colored paper and cut it up and made $10, $5, and $1 notes and labeled all our products with prices. When our mall was ready to open, we went looking for customers. We happened to live on a street where we knew many kids, so we didn't have to look very far. Many of the children came, and toured our new mall and shopped as we exchanged our parents' things for the fake money we made. Shoppers loaded their newfound treasures into old plastic grocery bags we had and during our climax of creative foolishness, they took our parents' things home.

We cleared our mall by the time mom and dad got home, and they found us innocently sitting in front of the television with our caregiver in the kitchen preparing dinner, completely unaware of what had happened. Mom greeted us headed for her bedroom to change and walked past my brother's room stopped and obviously noticed something was wrong because nothing was in place by her standards.

Mom called us both and asked what we spend the day doing. My brother was fearful of the consequences and pulled out the fake money he had in his pocket and went on to rat on us. I don't think I have ever seen my mother so angry, she yelled my father's name and told him what happened and blamed our behavior on his family and his genes. Dad's reaction was a little better than mom's. He took one look at the room, then at us and laughed and said wow, these kids are smart! Well a censored version of what happened after that is that we had to go door to door and apologize to the other kids' parents' and collect all the items we sold and return home with them.

Growing up we also loved to watch reruns of the Olympics; we often recorded them on those videocassettes from the '90s. One time we decided we would have our own Olympics in our backyard and invite the children on our street to participate. We planned a triathlon, consisting of running, cycling (for those who had bicycles) and swimming. Our swimming pool had no water, my father had drained it earlier that month because of a serious mosquito infestation but that did not stop us from finding a hosepipe and secretly filling it with water over a few days (fortunately we could swim). While having our Olympic day, and to our horror, dad decided to come home early during the day, which was not often, and he found us swimming in a pool full of water he had taken out, with our neighbor's kids! Dad calmly told us to get out of the pool and hardly said a word, he told the other kids to go home, and then asked us to follow him into the house. He did not say a word to us until mom came home, mom yelled as usual, but dad made a phone call and our punishment was to go spend the rest of our summer holiday at Grandpa's house (he knew we feared Grandpa). The next day we were put on a bus and shipped to Grandpa's house. We hated visiting Grandpa because he was a principal at a school and a serious advocate for discipline, he and Grandma were English teachers and avid readers. When we arrived, we were given a strict summer reading program, allowed no television and were supervised at all times. Even in the midst of this difficult situation, we found a way to relieve ourselves creatively.

Grandpa had a series of books in his home bookshelf that many kids in schools were reading. He had many of the latest releases since he was a teacher so we managed to convince him when it was time to return home to let us take the books for "academic betterment" purposes. He loaned us the books, but when we returned home we secretly started renting the books to other children in the neighborhood and the proceeds obviously went to a worthy cause, our personal ice cream and sweets fund. Business was booming until my father found out and we had to hand over our profits and the books back to Grandpa and apologize.

I share all these stories to share the fact that as children we are innately curious and creative but as we become adults we often lose that innocence. When my brother and I were getting up to our regular shenanigans, my parents thought we were rebellious but as we have gotten older they realize we were just innovative creative kids with an entrepreneurial spirit but no outlet.

Children have the benefit of not knowing that something is impossible. When I think about some of my childhood "adventures" I always saw the possibilities and no failure or consequence. In transitioning into adulthood I seemed to lose the intensity of the creative vibe I had as a child, and all I know is the law, compliance, restrictions and regulations, boundaries, rejection, humiliation and failure became the filter I created through. Everything I thought about attempting as a child demanded discovery, but adulthood demands conformity and responsibility. It's important to have fun! Never lose your sense of adventure and your sense of play. Children know how to play; and creative adventures and curiosity comes from being playful.

A Lesson from Children

When I served as a Children's ministry Bible class teacher, I taught over 250, 3-5-year olds every Sunday for 5 years. (I can gladly say that I lived to tell the story … lol). It was a sea of curious, excited little eyes and mouths that had endless questions. I was often asked, "Miss Chipo, what is that?

Why do we have to do that? Why does that person have that on? Why is this leader on their phone?" I often silenced them with a treat when I was just about ready to pull out my hair.

During the week, when I was not teaching the children, it bothered me that I did not have answers for all their questions. I realized that because of my age and over time, I had become so comfortable with my surroundings that I had stopped seeing them through the curious and innocent eyes of a child. I stopped questioning everything around me.

Children between the ages of 3-5 create with intention, and by the time they are 5, they add details and words to what their imaginations conceive. Children at this age love to play pretend games, experiment and explore. They recognize that art and ideas can tell a story. I think as adults we become so set in our ways, we don't want to change. As we age, we start to form "ruts" in our ways of thinking. We accept that things ought to be this way, and stop questioning why things are the way they are.

I recently read *Think Like a 5-Year Old*, by Len Wilson (2015). I loved what he had to say about the types of thinking children and adults engage in. Children tend to engage in thinking patterns that are full of imagination, surprise, invention, discovery, provocation and prediction. Adults tend to think more about responsibilities. They tend to focus more on evaluation, knowledge, deduction, judgment, criticism, and assessment. Generally, everyone engages in both types of thinking, and they are complimentary. However, with age, we tend to engage far less in childlike creative thinking than when we are children.

One thing I cherish about children is that they often see further than what they can pay for, just like the little boy who had the two fishes and five loaves saw the potential of his lunch, instead of the problem of the 5,000. I find it hard to believe that in a company of 5,000 men, not one of them had lunch or money to get lunch. I wonder if maybe he was the only one brave enough to share what he had. I recall that many things I often thought about doing as a child were things I could not pay for, but I was determined to do them anyway. A great example would be the story I shared about the book rental business I started.

Some folks can have so much creativity brewing on the inside, but no outlet to express it. They end up frustrated sometimes—releasing negative behaviors and emotions because they are not sure what to do with themselves. Everyone has been given the choice to either express constructive or destructive creativity and the power or will to choose. In sharing some of my fond memories my prayer is that you would cultivate and identify what you and your children (if you have any) are good at early on, and not reject and suppress it.

Getting an Education

"I think you need to get a professional degree, in life you always need to have something to fall back on and be able to pay your bills." Be careful; why don't you pick a more secure future for yourself? Don't venture on a creative path because you are guaranteed to starve. Too often, we hide from our true calling behind security. My father will admit because we can laugh about it, that for years he fought me about my pursuit for a career in the arts. He saw no future or substance in becoming a designer, and said I would have safety and security as an accountant.

I vividly remember in high school the day he found out that I had gone behind his back and chosen art classes as my core classes, instead of accounting and math as he had recommended. I was brilliant at accounting, but hated it. As I got older, I realized my father did not mean me any harm. He wanted me to have security, and he saw accounting providing that. But sometimes, when you have a dream that won't go away, there is always a part of you that wants to take a risk.

I will be honest though, that even in pursuing an education in the arts, there were a few things I could have done differently. One of which was following the crowd. I admit to getting an education because everyone else was doing it; but beyond this, I did not have a plan. School trains us to look for jobs and not create innovative things. Personally, I don't think education has made me more creative as I imagined it would. It has not made me thoughtful or more innovative or confident. If anything, it has made me literate, provided me with technical skills that have helped me become more analytical and a better communicator.

At the 2005 Stanford Commencement, Steve Jobs said something that set fireworks off in my mind. He described how he had dropped several classes and only attended the ones he felt he would benefit from. He decided to take a typography and calligraphy class, where he learned about Serifs and Sans Serif, and varying spaces between letter combinations. He learned how typography was "beautiful, historical, and artistically subtle," and none of the classes had any practical relevance to his life.

However, 10 years later, what he learned in this class influenced how they designed the Mac. The Mac's design and typography was heavily influenced by the classes he took in typography and calligraphy; and as a result, they created the first computer with beautiful typography.

If he had never dropped out of the required classes, he never would have dropped into that Typography and Calligraphy class that contributed to his journey of innovation. There are classes I benefited a lot from, but it was the ones that taught me skills like the ones Steve Jobs described that added value to what I do.

In some industries, what matters is your output, not what you studied. What you produce is more valuable than the degree you have, for example this applies in industries for entrepreneurs, technology professionals, freelancers and those in the entertainment industry. Some of your customers won't care where you went to school, but they do care whether or not you can deliver an excellent product or service. I know others may disagree here and that is okay; this is just my personal view. Sadly, we live in a world that is full of creative people and some are preoccupied with academic accomplishment with a trail of degrees. But statistics show that many people, who are overqualified, cannot find jobs.

A Creative Flavor that Counts

Traditional rules and thinking are made to be broken. I have decided to fully blossom and have purposed in my heart to experience the happiness and fulfillment I was created to experience. I have a flavor to contribute that nobody else has. This ought to be enough reason for me to do something. In the past I thought in order to be creative I had to come up with something different—something nobody had ever done. But I don't think that anymore. I think being creative is just being you. It is important to have the confidence that what God has given you is so valuable, and that God gave it to you because He already has confidence in you. God gives you creative ideas because He has confidence in you, and that is also His way of extending an exclusive invitation to you. "God does not give anything without expecting anything back" (Oral Roberts).

I am reminded of the scripture in Luke 12:36, "… to whom much is given, much is required." God giving you creative ideas is Him putting His favor on you and letting you know that He is up to something. There is value in taking the time to pray and to find out who you are. Value is not determined by what you have, but by Who is dwelling inside of you.

CHAPTER SIX
A HERITAGE
OF CREATIVITY

"I have inherited Your testimonies forever,
For they are the joy of my heart"
(Psalm 119:111).

Africans are irrepressible. Coming from Africa I felt like I needed to throw in a chapter on my heritage and the creative environment I come from. Africa has been called the Dark Continent, but it is a place teeming with creative potential, so much so that I prefer to refer to it as the Bright Continent.

I loved growing up on African soil, and what I learnt was that you quickly learn the art of improvising. We have many problems in Africa, but it amazes me how so many people are able to use their scarcity for innovation. Africans are by nature problem solvers, and even with little or no access to technology, we know how to make a plan. The recent widespread accessibility to Smartphones and the Internet is breaking stereotypical and geographical boundaries. Innovators are being birthed who are becoming literary champions, film festival award winners, street children who are going on to become Oscar winners or Harvard graduates, contemporary jazz musicians, fashion designers, scientists, entertainers, culinary crafters, musicians and entrepreneurs. There is an enormity of talent, but sadly, there are many who are not profiting the way they should from their innovations in Africa.

I feel a little homesick as I have nostalgic, fond

memories of endless rows of busy booths, kiosks, stalls and tables with women selling every imaginable thing from raw vegetables to handcrafted baskets. The funny thing is, it is often women selling exactly the same thing lined up next to each other, competing for the same customers. The women still manage to hustle and make something at the end of the day in that dusty, fly-infested market with people everywhere. To these busy businesswomen, presentation is important, and items must be visually pleasing, especially if it is fabric, jewelry or raw vegetables. The key to success is to show up every-day, and have an excellent sense of customer service.

Africans are not lazy or idle people, everyone is busy, but what is heartbreaking is even though everyone is a business person, many still live in the stench and squalor in townships, slums, remote villages or the bush because of infrastructure underdevelopment and a lack of access to technological advancement and educational opportunities. In many places in Africa, people live in survival mode, where the norm is to spend the entire day trying to stay alive.

Creative Awakening

When I moved to the United States as a student, my eyes were opened to many opportunities, but the eye-opening was bittersweet because it made what we did not have back home more apparent. I thought of the crafters, sculptors, and basket weavers in the markets. Some of their pieces are sold for as low as a $1 a piece, even though they spent days working on them. Many times, their work is often brought here and resold for thousands of dollars. A lack of intellectual and property knowledge has really put us at a disadvantage, often we don't know the value of what we have.

Learning in an environment where you can interact with people from different nations really opens your eyes to things you may have overlooked. I quickly learned that in some countries creativity is undervalued, unidentified and ignored because it is seen as a luxury and not as a necessity. Back home we have many unusual policies and regulations that do not protect artists or support our creative capabilities, also the issues of corruption do not help. The heartbreaking realization I had was that sitting and dreaming is a luxury some cannot afford, and for others it's a reality they cannot live without.

I stand hopeful though because Africans are problem solvers. We know we have a creative heritage. My prayer is that more Africans would get opportunities for education, and improved infrastructure and technology. This may be a bit random, but I was a little shocked when I looked up how many cinemas there were in Africa compared to the United States. I found an estimate of less than 1,000 in Africa and about 41,000 in the United States (Dahir, Abdi Latif. 2017). These margins scared me, and I realized how much further ahead other countries were. I pray for our mindset that as a people we would know what to do with opportunities because sometimes even with all the opportunities in the world a poverty mindset will always take us backward instead of forward.

A Creative Economy

Creativity is the new gold on the African continent. Africa is in a season where the time is ripe for the manifestation of many things God wants to do. There are many God is raising up to solve problems on multiple levels in Africa, with clever and affordable solutions. I am moved by how there are many African musicians who play by ear and can't even read music. It is a skill that has been passed down from generation to generation. The African entertainment and music industry is oozing with mind-blowing talent. My prayer is that we would know what to do with all the gifts God has given.

One of my favorite cities in America is Nashville Tennessee, the city that has exploded on a foundation of music. Music in Nashville is the thread that connects the artists, the city and the people. Nashville is known as the "Songwriting Capital of the World" and many songwriters come to the Music City from all over the world to learn the art. There is even a Songwriters Festival in Nashville.

But what makes the city a gem in Tennessee is that what happens goes beyond the beat. It is about musicians building community in Nashville. The music industry there works because of a harmonious relationship between innovation, business and music. This creates an environment that helps musicians thrive. There are opportunities to connect career with community, entrepreneurship training with social causes and support to help other artists through a peer community.

Stereotypically in Africa, musicians and artists today make music because they want to be famous, want to make money, or want to gain the attention and praises of the masses. There are musicians who have a broader perspective, but even more need to be motivated to build their community and their continent. I would like to see policies in Africa that help sustain musicians and artists. An example would be to develop arts districts that provide display, studio, and performance spaces for visual and performing arts or industry experts that genuinely care about, value, and would be willing to pay for the craft of songwriting. Imagine if the governments in Africa were able to foster international music themed festivals, museums and tourism through economic development that had a tolerance to inspire creativity? And, what if more cities in Africa embraced music and artistry as legitimate and valid career choices that were worthy of attention and funding?

In most places in Africa you still get the follow up question, "Yeah, but what do you do for work?" which can dampen the enthusiast newbie musicians who cannot seem to get the same level of understanding and respect that musicians get in a city like Nashville. Music is in the DNA of Nashville, and that creates a platform for many musicians in a number of ways. Music produced in Nashville generates over one billion dollars in revenue annually, and for every 1,000 working, 20-64 year olds living in Nashville, there are 7.8 music industry jobs (the next highest is Los Angeles which only has 2.8 jobs per 1,000 residents) (Pollack, 2015).

In Africa we need less fragmentation and more cluster innovation where industries or specific ideas that are popular are concentrated in certain areas for community and support systems. "Nashville is the city that listens, and we listen to all kinds of music here" (Tumminello). My desire is that all cities in Africa would listen to what God is creating and doing through the many creative people who are yet to be discovered.

In the Atmosphere

There is no such thing as a Christian chord and a secular chord in music. A chord is a chord. God is all about atmospheres, and creativity thrives in an atmosphere of creativity. An atmosphere of creativity pulls creativity out, and an atmosphere of true worship pulls true worship out. There is a hymn called, *A Mighty Fortress Is Our God*, and the writer heard the tune while they were sitting in a tavern (which would translate to a modern day bar). I am not condoning going to a bar to get inspired to write the next hymn. The point I want to make is that the writer sat in the tavern and heard a tune and said, "There is a song in the tune that had not been written yet."

There are many tunes out there, but it's the words that give the tune power. A tune is just made up of notes, chords and rhythms. In the Tower of Babel incidence, the people were speaking the same language, and using the same words in Genesis 11:1. There was a harmony in speaking and saying the same thing, and God said, "Nothing they set out to do will be impossible for them" (vs 6). There was a pleasant atmosphere, and creativity is birthed in an atmosphere that is harmonic.

In any form of creativity, there is something about being in the atmosphere. Saul got in the company of prophets and began to prophesy. He was not even a prophet, but because he was caught up in the atmosphere, he started speaking the same language as those who were called to prophesy. When you get in the atmosphere, something happens, whether it is in fashion, music, photography, business, film, or writing. What happens in that atmosphere can begin to spawn and multiply. I think that is why many musicians thrive in Nashville, because they get caught up in the atmosphere of creative musical prowess, where many musicians gather and are trained.

The Importance of Value

I had an interesting encounter with a Zulu vendor on my last visit home at a jewelry market in South Africa. I was thoroughly impressed by the attention to detail and craftsmanship of the African Zulu beaded jewelry some of the vendors were selling. The pieces I saw were all handcrafted, and some women sat behind their stalls, busily creating new pieces by hand in the scorching heat. I started to talk to one of the ladies about her work and how creative I thought she was. I asked her if she had thought about having her own website. The lady laughed hysterically with a lady at a neighboring stall. She then said something about me in Zulu I did not understand.

I was not offended by her reaction, but more so surprised and disappointed that she had already decided to exclude herself from that kind of progress. She thought that only an "anointed" group of people could create and have a thriving business and website. She was just in it to survive and have enough money for bus fare, to pay her bills and buy more beads for tomorrow's hustle. Creating anything is a process, but sadly, the reality is often that different people engage the process on different levels. The Zulu vendor lady failed to see her contribution to the process of creating anything that was valuable. There was no one else putting value on her work because she did not value it herself.

I understand this firsthand—creating anything artistic

is not easy. You invest time, energy, ideas and make yourself vulnerable by putting yourself out there, not knowing how people are going to react or respond to what you have made. There is an investment of my senses—my hands have contact with what I craft, and I am not just offering an object, but an experience. I am giving people an opportunity to experience my intellect and my heart. You never know how valuable what God has hidden in what you choose to do and choose to value.

Ideas Out of Crisis

I appreciate many things about my African heritage, one of which is that ideas that I've had have often come out of crisis. A crisis is a perfect climate for creativity because you are forced out of your comfort zone. Some visual connections I had growing up made little sense at the time, and because of my environment, I instinctively knew how relationships worked with colors, shapes, space and other design elements. However, when I attended art and design school, the education gave me a whole new outlook on the creative process. I realized that some of the visual observations and connections I had were not coincidences. My creative eye was trained by my experiences, and I saw things about growing up in Africa that were always firing in my mind.

I put resources together for steps to consider before embarking on a quest for creative adventures. I think some of these are very close to home for me. I remember making mistakes when I started my business. If anything, I am becoming more intentional about my self-awareness, my priorities, having a positive mindset, being a wise decision maker, managing my time, building relationships, and developing my educational and mental growth. Here are a few nuggets I picked up while watching those who have succeeded where I am trying:

1. Attach meaning to what you create.

Let's be honest. When your funds are dry, any idea

that will bring in a little income is worth the try, right? I used to think that way, a lot; fortunately, I did not venture into any "sticky" money-making ventures. Meaning adds value to what you create; it also helps you stay focused, whether the money is flowing or that river is dry. I like what Bishop T.D. Jakes says, "Focus on Purpose not Profit". (Bishop T.D. Jakes, Soar, 2017). Meaning is not always a spiritual connection. Sometimes, God will have you and I create something that will be a resource that can advance the work of the Kingdom. A good example is inventing a household product that can be used by everyone. In this context, the meaning would come from what you do with the money you get from this invention. For example, helping orphans or buildings homes for those who need help.

2. Passion should partner with patience.

Everything worth creating takes time. Sometimes, God loves us enough to take the time to dig and put a steady foundation in us that will know how to weather the storms when they come. Just because your idea is not as far ahead as someone else's, it doesn't mean it's not going anywhere. Sometimes, the lesson and the test are in the wait.

3. Your competition has innovation valleys you can learn from.

When I look at my competition, I am not intimidated by them; instead, I focus on an opportunity to learn from them. There are creative opportunities to be found in what others have taken for granted, overlooked or ignored. I used to think innovation could only come through creating something that had never been done before. Some ideas are pioneered, and others are refined. There isn't one way to innovate and come up with something creative. Creative innovation can come in so many ways through a product, a lyric, networking, an experience, a service, or a relationship.

4. Don't fear failure.

"Failure sucks, but instructs." - David Kelley

"Failure is a bruise not a tattoo" (Sinclair). Prototypes and failures are part of the process. Sometimes, our lives are full of the things that hold us hostage. I have days I just need to avoid what feeds fear in my life. It is often a huge blessing to abandon the crowd. When I fail it's okay because that failure is taking me one step closer to and not further away from my creative goal. Harvard turned Warren Buffet down, and he says that was the best thing that happened to him—what was ahead of him was better because of what happened to him. It is better to fail as a skilled master at something than to be like the person who has never even tried anything. Accepting failure and learning from it helps me to grow, but accepting it and not trying does more harm than good for my life.

5. Everything in life is an opportunity.

The conversations we have, events we attend, encounters with strangers, the things we watch and read, the victories and valleys are all opportunities to grow and discover something that we did not know. Listening is a great opportunity, the art of being a good listener is something we often take for granted because we want to and are trying so hard to be heard. In every encounter I have daily, I try to listen with all my senses and connect the information I am hearing to the relationship. It has helped me become a better creative communicator to observe tone, body language and emotion. Curiosity can make listening easier.

Sometimes there are instances where we need to step back from what we know to pursue what we don't know. Abraham, aka "Abe," went through this painful but necessary transition. God had to take him out of what he knew so he could possess what he didn't know. (Genesis 12:1).

PART 3
OTHER'S IMAGE

CHAPTER SEVEN
CREATED FOR
A MUTUAL ADVANTAGE

"Let nothing be done through selfish ambition or conceit,
but in lowliness of mind let each esteem others better than himself.
Let each of you look out not only for his own interests,
but also for the interests of others"
(Philippians 2:3-4).

There is a hotel in America known for its impeccable service. The company has a policy where the employees are all assigned $2,000 to spend on a guest per incident. The concept behind the $2,000 is for employees to do something to create a meaningful experience for a guest staying at the hotel. The reason behind the $2,000 is that the money is used not just to solve a problem, but also to create an outstanding experience.

I wonder how different the world would be, if everyone could remember that God assigned all of us with "$2,000" to help others have an outstanding experience of His unsearchable love for us. In Christian circles, we know we have been created in the image of God, but we quickly forget that others, especially those who have hurt and offended us, and those still living in sin, were created in the image of God, too. God created us with equal value, and equal dignity. Often, when people serve a greater purpose, going the extra mile is not burdensome. It's easy to find your creative purpose once you are ready to look behind the clutter of selfishness.

Creativity has a mutual advantage, for the one creating

and the one benefiting from the thing that has been created. It is important to create value. I know that my 'go-to' businesses have created so much value, and they are officially obvious choices. Creating value not only adds value to my mission, but it also creates a meaningful experience for others. Valuing what I do is so important. If I don't see the value in it, nobody else will, either. It is hard to see the value of what I create, especially when it comes so naturally. I cannot tell you the number of times I shortchanged myself in the past because I could not see how valuable my craft was because it came "naturally" to me.

How Much Do I Owe You?

God has a way of leading us out of the wilderness of foolishness, and I sure am glad He leads me away from it to wisdom. I remember an encounter I had several years ago with a Swiss gentleman. He had asked me to create a handcrafted greeting card for someone he was close to for their birthday. I created a 4.5 (11.4 cm) by 5.5 inch (13.97 cm) card. It was small, but I spent days designing a three dimensional wire and glass beaded flower that I attached to the card. I know I am probably not doing justice to how intricate the card was, but I put my heart into what I created. When I presented the card to him he took a long look at it, and because of his long silence, I panicked and thought, "My work was probably shoddy by his standards."

He stared at the card in silence and then broke the long silence with, "How much do I owe you?" My response was, "Um … whatever you think it's worth." He looked at me slightly offended and said, "How much do you think your work is worth?" A little uncomfortable, I responded, "$15," and then quickly coughed out, "Or maybe $10, since you don't seem happy with it." He shook his head—a little alarmed and said, "You want me to pay $10 for this card? Are you serious Chipo?" (At this point, I was ready to crawl into a hole with my card and disappear.)

He then sat me down and said, "Chipo, this card is not worth $15; it's not even worth $10; the beadwork, the paper, how long did this even take you to make? I refuse to pay $10 for this. I am giving you $300." Shock is an understatement of my reaction as he pulled out $300 for a greeting card! The lesson I learned was how important it is to own the value of my work, and that it can create a ripple effect around me. If I don't value my work, neither will anyone else.

I make a difference; what I create can solve a problem. I believe that all forms of expression are valuable. What I create is valuable because it compels others to think, to feel and to love. My ideas help to express emotions and bring stories to life. When you do, what you love and you are passionate and make other people happy, that is adding value.

The Creative Wedge

Get around other value-driven creators to develop a value mindset. I watched a video of geese flying in a v shape (a wedge) the other day. I became curious and started reading about geese. It turns out that the reason geese fly together is it provides additional life and reduces air resistance for the other geese flying behind in the same V wedge. The wedge is important because the whole flock can fly 70% farther with the same energy than a goose flying alone. Geese in the wedge can get to their destination faster and with less energy extended in the wedge. Surrounding myself with the right people often comes with opportunities to learn from their victories and their failures.

A goose that leaves the wedge often has to exert more energy in trying to reach its destination alone. Flying solo can be frustrating, stressful and lonely. I have tried to do things solo and missed the synergy, connection, accountability, and growth. De-cluttering and finding my purpose is easier when I get into a value "wedge" and surround myself with those who are on the same mission I am.

The creative wedge helps in two ways. I have accountability for my actions and I have an example to learn from and people to throw my creative ideas off of. I had a spiritual mentor in my life who I cherish and learned so much from. I used to share everything with them, but I felt like I was starting to drain them because I went to them for everything, spiritual, emotional, ideas, business, education, finances, goals, everything. I was asking them for advice in areas they were not experienced in. It is impossible to go at it with just one other person; your creative wedge needs more than one person for it to be effective.

God is bringing a creative wedge of people I trust and who add value to my craft by coaching and helping me in the areas I need to grow. I have quickly learned that there are safe and unsafe people in my life. Just because someone is unsafe doesn't mean they are a bad person. They are just not a go-to person for my ideas. I loved something Bishop T.D. Jakes said once, "There are three categories of supporters you will encounter in life. The distant people, who do not validate who you are, the inner circle that is allowed to see you sweat, and the divine who we can be intimately close to and find healing. When you have an idea, don't confuse your creative wedge with your fans. Having a creative wedge has helped me define my seven P's:

- my **plan**
- my **passion**
- my **purpose**
- my **priorities**
- keeps me **positive**
- strengthens my **persuasion**
- identifies the **people** I need to connect with

The other day I had a fond memory about a college I attended. Many millionaires' kids attended the same private college. Often, they went to Switzerland, Paris, Japan or other countries for the weekend. An important lesson I learned while studying there was that their thinking and priorities were different. The parents had a different approach to the goals they had for their kids attending college. These parents often encouraged their kids to have good grades and get around the right people—people who furthered their goals and contacts. Every relationship they had they saw as an opportunity to succeed or fail, and they taught their kids to build a social and relational infrastructure that would bless them in the future and add value to their dreams. I was grateful to have this kind of wedge at this stage of my life as a student, because I also learned to find my own voice, as I was often called on in class and forced to take a stand on my values and articulate my thoughts.

Grapes and Humility

I mention the story about the spies going to see the Promise Land and the cluster of grapes they brought back to show the Israelites. I was eating a bowl of grapes recently and thinking about the fact that being in a creative wedge helps to keep you humble. I looked up the Hebrew words for grape and humility, and the word is the same, "ah nav." I know you are thinking, "What do grapes have to do with humility?" A grape has no importance as a single grape; nobody buys single grapes, and grapes are bought in clusters. The connection I saw was that a humble person is one who sees no self-importance by doing everything alone, but they share their life with others.

Creativity and Money

It is amazing how many quote scripture, but don't experience scripture. I used to look at my condition and immediately decide that my portion in life was to be in proportion to my condition. But Jesus came that we might have life and have it more abundantly. Jesus died to restore everything God intended for us to have. He also died to ensure we would not experience and accept things that would mock

His redemptive power.

Money is a sensitive issue in the Church. I have been one of the culprits who confessed that the wealth of the wicked was laid out for the righteous, but that wealth is laid out for the righteous men and women who are willing to practice the principles of financial management in the Kingdom of God. God does not operate on our emotions, but He operates on His Word and on principles. A frustration I have had about being creative in church; is in the church I learned how to pray. I learned about the Word of God, but I didn't learn management principles about money. If I am not fortunate enough to be around financially savvy friends or have a business degree, it is hard to find information on financing your ideas and financial management from within the church. There are churches that are starting to realize this and are making efforts to change, but it is very few that have grasped how important these principles are to ministry and business.

In the church, making disciples is the currency and reproducing makes Heaven rejoice. But God wants us to fulfill this call with all of our resources properly stewarded. Sometimes, God will provide supernaturally for your vision, and other times, God will give you a plan. God gave Joseph a supernatural interpretation of pharaoh's dreams that led to Joseph being promoted from a prisoner to the governor of Egypt. Joseph, however, came up with the plan of what Egypt would do to preserve and manage what they had in the season of famine.

Information is important to ideas. It is important to sit down and measure or estimate the cost (Luke 14:28). How much will it cost? How much do I have? Do I know anyone who can help me come up with a financial plan? It is important to get the financial information you need to start your venture, but it has to be quality information because sometimes poor quality information or too much information can lead you to indecision or no progress.

One of my prayer points in this season is for God to

remove all the unconsciously passed down, limiting beliefs that I was taught about money. A good way to do this is to connect through a relationship with someone who is thriving—where you are trying to go. We are taught how to work hard, borrow and save. The fear of being without money often drives some people to work, and they work to seek safety, have comfort and avoid pain. It is a little dangerous and frustrating to be directed by security and not passion. Righteous living and intentionally applying Divine biblical principles for handling wealth can break the hold of poverty on the life of any Christian. There is a reason the Bible says, "I am come that you might have life and have it more abundantly" (John 10:10), and that "the earth is the Lord's and the fullness thereof" (Psalm 24:1). God can renew the mind of someone who is ready to make necessary changes to experience the favor, prosperity, and provision He intended for all of us to have.

If God can pull a coin out of a fish, He can pull what you need out for the fulfillment and manifestation of the dream He has written on your heart. There are industries that focus on the love of money. Sadly, money takes on the form and personality of the one who possesses it. The need for your idea can be taken care of by God. He can provide and will provide so you can stay pure and focused on God and not on money. Asaph never had a need, they had to flow in the things of God so much that God always made sure their needs were met. God wanted them to stay in the flow of His presence.

A Good Fire

Breakthrough does not come from the army, but if you can find a group or an individual who can give your work the attention it deserves, this can make a huge difference. It just took One Man to change the daily grind of the disciples. They were washing their nets in Luke 5:2-11 and had already left the boat because they had not caught anything. Jesus got into Simon's boat and started teaching from the boat. When

He was done, He instructed Simon Peter to let down his nets into the "deep water." The disciples caught more fish that day than they had ever caught in their entire career because of an encounter they had with Jesus.

A few years ago, I read about the Inklings. (Jeschke, Melanie M., 2004.) A literary group that included Tolkien, C. S. Lewis, and Charles Williams. These writers formed a fellowship of the imagination that later inspired imaginative writings. These were notable writers, who would get together and read their works in progress to each other. They gave some pretty intense but encouraging critiques to one another. Lewis once wrote about the group, "Is there any pleasure on earth as great as a circle of good friends by a good fire?"

I am on a quest for a "good fire." There is nothing more inspiring than being able to sit and fellowship with those on a similar mission with a deep passion. When Jesus had the Last Supper, the multitudes could not be there. There was only a select 12 who were chosen to fellowship in preparation of His passion (Matthew 26:17- 30). The Inklings literary group critiques led to stretching many of the members creative muscles and the birthing of work we all read and love today, including *The Lord of the Rings* and *the Chronicles of Narnia*. Diana Glyer calls this group of individuals, "resonators." They help affirm you and guide you back when you are off track.

A Lesson from Hemingway

Hemingway the Paris Years is a must-read, and I was intrigued by Ernest Hemingway's story in the book. Ernest Hemingway started out as a writer with some notable talent, but he did not have the kind of exposure he had later in his career. When he was in Chicago, he met Sherwood Anderson who encouraged him to relocate to Paris. Sherwood was convinced that a move to Paris would expose Hemingway to a community of writers and other creative's through Gertrude Stein, who led the group. (Reynolds, Michael S., 1989).

Hemingway moved to Paris, and while he was there, he met James Joyce, as well as other notable writers. This led to connections with notable publishers. The connections he made in Paris helped change the course of his career forever. He was immersed in the craft of writing in Paris, and spent much time around other notable writers, who started to rub off on him. Hemingway went on to become one of the most famous writers of the 20th century. Creative work cannot happen in isolation; sometimes it needs a creative wedge to endure. Having a network can help your work mature more quickly. Meaningful creative connections are there, and more resources than we know of are available, if we are willing to look. The more opportunities we allow ourselves to connect with the right people, the greater our chances to stand in the presence of greatness, and the more likely that greatness will rub off on us.

The Secret Megalopolis of the Ant World

Ants are everywhere, and we generally think very little of them. Ants bite and can be a real nuisance when they creep into your pantry or gate crash at your picnic; I have often squashed them without noticing as they marched around on sidewalks. Ants seem insignificant yet the bible tells us to study and learn from ants, that we are to consider their ways, and be wise. (Proverbs 6:6) After all, God often uses the foolish things to shame the wise. (1 Corinthians 1:27)

When observed, ants are always busy, working, and no one tells them what to do or coerces them to work. Ants also plan for the future, work in community and can often carry weight that is 10 - 50 times their own body weight. In the ant world; ants are soldiers, nurses, highway construction workers and sanitation specialists in the ant kingdom. Every ant counts, and ants do not distinguish between good and bad performing ants, they simply place the right ants in the right job. Ants teach each other to work and hold each other accountable.

Several years ago in a Biology class, I watched a documentary about Leaf ants from Brazil that built sophisticated underground cities that have been compared to the Great Wall of China. (Gavaghan, 2012) There is one particular colony that was discovered in 2010 and it featured paths and gardens, subterranean highways and tunnels, and it housed one of the biggest leaf cutter ant colonies in the world.

Ten tonnes of concrete were poured on the surface of the ground that had served as breathing air ducts for the ants and the concrete completely filled the ducts. It took the scientists ten days to pour the concrete down the channels until they actually filled up, that is how deep the channels in the ground created by the millions of ants were. The colony covered an area of 500sq ft (46.45sq meters) and was 26ft (7.725 meters) deep. Scientists kept digging and discovered this hidden city that was built by the leaf ants, and they excavated 40 tonnes of soil, which featured scores of highways, main routes and side roads underground.

When ants cooperate they build amazing things, this Brazilian ant colony underground was so intricate it looked like it was created by an architect. It took weeks to uncover this formidable fortress, and the scientists removed tonnes of earth to reach it. The huge network of tunnels was once populated by literally millions of leaf cutter ants that managed to coordinate themselves to build this incredible city.

There is a lot we can learn from ants, and what is intriguing about them is that they are smarter together than they are alone. The intelligence of ants as a community is a wonder; and it is fascinating to watch ants manage their own complex societies right under our noses! Ants have a wonderful sense of direction, they don't just gather for themselves, but they were created with a "social stomach" that can store food for other ants left at the colony when they go out looking for food. (Dussutour and Simpson, 2009)

I long for a creative community that is open to share information, there are instances where as humans we are inclined to be vague and withhold valuable information and wisdom that would help others avoid the mistakes we have made. I have had personal experiences where I knew people who had information that would help me but they were not willing to share the information. I don't know if it is something in our human nature that has a tendency to do that, but much is to be learnt from ants that value the importance of community and shared ideas with other ants in their colony and how they can have mutual benefit from what they know and what they have.

Lessons Learned in Mutual Advantage

There is much to be learned when you surround yourself with the right people about creativity. Creative people tend to have some traits:

1. They observe everything - keep a notebook close by.
2. They take time to tap into the Essence of who they are - constructive solitude is a time to stop and listen to God. You need to be connected with God to express Who He is.
3. They seek out new experiences - intellectual curiosity is a daily must.
4. They ask the big questions - why and how are necessary.
5. They watch others - some of our best ideas and inspiration can come from here.
6. They are not afraid to imagine - some of my best ideas come when my mind is wondering.
7. They see their places of pain as places of power.
8. They fail.
9. They do what they are passionate about.
10. They let go of the present and grab hold of the possibilities of the future.

11. They see possibilities where others see only problems.

12. They surround themselves with those who inspire them.

CHAPTER EIGHT
CREATE?!
WHAT IF THEY
DISAPPROVE?

*"And the one also who had received the one talent came
up and said, 'Master, I knew you to be a hard man, reaping
where you did not sow and gathering where you scattered no
seed. And I was afraid, and went away and hid your talent
in the ground. See, you have what is yours.'*

*"But his master answered and said to him, 'You wicked,
lazy slave, you knew that I reap where I did not sow and
gather where I scattered no seed. Then you ought to have
put my money in the bank, and on my arrival I would have
received my money back with interest.*

*"'Therefore take away the talent from him, and give it to
the one who has the ten talents. For to everyone who has,
more shall be given, and he will have an abundance; but
from the one who does not have, even what he does have
shall be taken away'"*
(Matthew 25:14-30).

    I tried to imagine how the servant with the one talent
felt, compared to the servant with ten talents and two talents.
He may have gone and hidden his talent because he compared
himself to the others, and compared to them, what he had to
offer would not amount to anything. In high school, I often
compared myself to girls that I thought were more talented

or had more than I did. Fear drove me to hide who I was and what I was capable of, just like the man with the single talent. He only had one talent, but even that one talent was important. It wasn't because of the value he or others put on it; it was because of Who it came from. If God created room for you and me to live in this world, there is plenty of room for every idea, vision and dream He puts in our hearts.

Great Ideas that were Rejected

History has shown us that any great idea like Shadrack, Mesheck and Abednego had had to face the furnace of disapproval and rejection. Here is a list of a few inventions we use everyday that either first failed or were ridiculed, but they went on to change the world:

The light bulb
Television
Airplanes
The telephone
Automobiles
Spacecraft
Personal computers
Cell phones
Online shopping

David Sarnoff Associates said, "The wireless music box has no imaginable commercial value. Who would pay for a message sent to nobody in particular?" (Craig-Purcel, Wendy, 2009.) In this conversation, they were rejecting the idea and proposal for the radio in the 1920s. Western Union said in an internal memo in 1876, "This "telephone" has too many shortcomings to be seriously considered as a means of communication. The device is inherently of no value to us." Today, although the use of the telephone has declined because of smartphones, there are more cell phones than people in the world, an estimate 7.19 billion! (2017 GSMA Intelligence digital analysts).

The aspirin idea was rejected, but today is the world's most popular pill; Americans swallowed an estimated 29 billion aspirins in 2004 (CBS NEWS, 2004). Sometimes your idea can be so far from the status quo that it can make people uncomfortable, and in a moment of uncertainty, they can reject you. Everyone wants to think they know the end of your story, but only God knows "when you sit and when you rise, and perceives your thoughts from afar" (Psalm 139:2). He knows what "no eye has seen, nor ear heard, nor have entered into the heart of man" the things He "has prepared for those who love Him" (1 Corinthians 2:9).

The creative things God puts in us are often rejected because those we present them to do not have a point of reference for who we really are. Do not be discouraged by the rejection; it just means you are onto something good! Sometimes our ideas are so far ahead, that it takes time for others to catch up with them. God can also often give you something that can cause you to be ahead of your time. The message Jesus preached about the Kingdom of God was ahead of the time that the laws the Pharisees were accustomed to. God called Noah to build something that was ahead of the time, yet the flood manifested. Everyone who saw the ark did not even know what to call what he was building. The prophetic dreams Joseph had were far ahead of the reality he was experiencing in his father's house. And the miracle that manifested through the Holy Spirit in Mary's womb was so far ahead of the wedding plans and marriage she and Joseph had for their lives.

Navigating Disapproval of Your Ideas

Our lives flourish when fertile things are born out of our minds. Every day we feed our minds with information to be able to stand with a deep enough conviction about the dream God puts in our hearts and minds, it is in choosing to be fed with the Word of God. I am dealing with this in this season:

learning to navigate the disapproval of others with my ideas.

Sometimes our circumstances dictate our choices. How we measure our own abilities affect how creative we think we are. Just the other day I spent hours thoughtfully creating a beautiful handcrafted purse. By my standards, it was a clever idea, functional, cute and something I knew someone else would totally rock. I took pictures of my latest creation and sent it to someone for their personal evaluation of my idea ... BIG MISTAKE! The response I got was, "This is definitely not something I would wear; I don't like it," and without thinking, I allowed their disapproval to sink in and erase what I had made and what it meant to me. I was ready to toss my idea in the garbage. Two days later after showing it to some other people, who loved it, I realized that just because they did not like it, did not mean everyone would not like it.

It's a crazy thing to imagine the number of things around us that govern our habits, our hearts and our heads. The battle is real, but every day it is in reminding myself that everything important to my life does not come from the opinions and disapproval of my critics. It starts with what I choose to consistently deposit in my head. I am deciding every day to do my future a favor by focusing on the right things today. The Bible says, "For as he thinketh in his heart, so is he ..." (Proverbs 23:7).

Criticisms are like mirrors. It is important to ask, "Do they actually reflect who you are? Or, do they contradict who God said you are?" Every day we engage in both spiritual and internal battles, and then we leave the house and have to deal with external battles when we present our ideas to people and they don't understand, don't get it, have prejudgments, think we are lazy, criticize us, reject us, laughed at us, shut us down, and think we are just weird. It is a lot to have to deal with when you are trying to gather the courage to start a creative venture.

The good news is that it is possible. Lately, I have been making it a habit to lean into the heart of God concerning what He wants to create and accomplish with my life. I am deliberately leaning out of the opinions and discouragement of others.

Mistakes that Keep
Creative Artists from Thriving

1. Neglecting the Power of Storytelling

Jesus used parables to tell stories with a deeper meaning.

"The world is not made of atoms.
It is made of stories" (Muriel Ruykeser).

2. Consistency and Discipline

I am so guilty of this one. I often hop from one idea to the next without laboring to fulfill or bring an idea to maturation. There is power in consistency and having the discipline to focus. It pays to possess the spirit of a finisher.

"Like a muscle, your creative abilities will grow and strengthen with practice." — **Tom Kelley**

3. Can't Handle Rejection

Rejection is part of the process; as long as there are people in the world, there will always be someone saying no.

4. Being Fearful of Thinking

Doers are great thinkers. Leonardo DaVinci was a great painter who mixed his own paints, studied anatomy, pigments, science (thinking) and art (doing). His ability to go beyond just doing and incorporating thinking and doing in his craft helped to make him stand out as a prolific artist.

A Creative Renewal

"And do not be conformed to this world, but be

transformed by the renewing of your mind..." because your mind will produce what you put in it. Most people have never had someone show them how to get out of their own way. Sometimes we are our own biggest hindrance to productivity. The place we often need to move out of the way in is what we often think of ourselves.

Our thoughts carry electromagnetic reality, and it is important to change what we think and imagine because this can easily bleed into our reality. Living in default mode can derail us from pursuing our God-given passion, the defaults of fear, confusion, lack of clarity, and the past. There are a few areas I have identified that can easily cause some people to fall into default mode:

1. Fear

The chief culprit, fear can be a huge hindrance to progress, and the worst thing we can do is to say, "I can't" without even trying. Fear is so powerful because it can usher you into inaction and time passes as you painfully realize you did nothing about your idea. There is only One Person who everyone should fear and that is God.

"The Lord is my light and my salvation;
whom shall I fear? The Lord is the strength of my life;
of whom shall I be afraid?" (Psalm 27:1).

2. Confusion

Having too many options can be counterproductive. Confusion comes from an inability to focus, and focusing is not just about saying yes, but about knowing what to say no to.

"For God is not a God of confusion but of peace ..."
(1 Corinthians 14:33).

3. A lack of clarity

I like for things to be clear before I endeavor on any

creative pursuit. I want to know how I am going to start and get to the final result—spontaneity is a struggle for me. I think it is important and beneficial to be clear about the starting point. The funny thing is the unexpected things always give us the most profound results. A great example is painting. I used to get so frustrated when I painted because no painting would turn out exactly the way I envisioned it. My frustration left when I discovered that what I expressed did not always look exactly like the original idea. The danger with wanting everything to make sense is the instinct to quit will kick in when something does not work out the way we planned. The hallmark of creativity is unpredictability, and sometimes you just have to respect the process (McNiff, Shaun, 1998).

4. The past

The past can be the biggest enemy to progress. The Word of God says,

"Forget the former things;
do not dwell on the past. See,
I am doing a new thing!
Now it springs up; Do you not perceive it?
I am making a way in the wilderness
And streams in the wasteland"
(Isaiah 43:18, 19).

It is often easier to stay in the past for fear of pursuing the uncertainty in the future. We know what the past looks like, we have tasted and experienced it, but we cannot do anything to change it. Instead, we can focus on changing the future, even though we are not certain of how it will look. I like how Stephen R. Covey puts it: "Live out of the imagination, not your history."

5. Unconscious passive experimenting

It is important to be in the moment and have

self-awareness. Passivity does not produce productivity.

"The purpose in a man's heart is like deep water,
but a man of understanding will draw it out"
(Proverbs 20:5).

I compiled a list of people who I care what they think. The list is very short and reading it over and over reminded me that most of the criticism I experience does not come from people on this list, but from everyone else.

I had some interesting conversations that lead me to compile a few thoughts of what to do differently when others disapprove. Sometimes we need to step back and ask:

1. Would I be better off if I listened to this person?

If your answer to this one is a resounding no, then I think you know what to do.

2. It's okay for people to have a different opinion than I do about my idea

The reality is we will never have everyone we know agree with us.

3. Take God at His Word. Don't take advice from people you are not willing to trade places with.

4. Ask the Holy Spirit to rewrite your rules for approval.

5. Don't react. Respond.

Reacting stems from a place of fear; responding comes from a position of trust.

6. Don't tell them, but show them.

Actions do really speak louder than words.

7. If that inner voice and prompting of the Holy Spirit has not said, "Listen to them," ... then don't.

A Lesson from Noah

The story about Noah is definitely one of my favorites. I feel a connection with Noah; I think because oftentimes a lot of things God tells me to do don't make any sense. Besides the fact that Noah was building something, he could not hide or explain, I cannot help but think about the comments and the rejection he went through from naysayers. I am sure he was the talk of the town, and a hot topic at everyone's dinner table. I wonder how Noah's family felt about what he was doing? Were they concerned about him? Did they think he was crazy? I wonder how many people tried to talk him out of what God said?

The one thing that really blew my mind about the ark Noah was building is that as far as we know it was not fitted with an engine. In order for that thing to move, it needed the power of God to move it. Noah had no compass, no sailing or building experience; we just know that he was a righteous man who had pleased God. Noah was not working with high tech equipment either. He had the primitive stuff. I doubt he had a crane, drill and a stash of nails lying around as well, or a local hardware store. I don't even think he had a place to test the ark to make sure it would float on water. I was a little curious and looked up the kind of wood Noah could have used. The Bible says it was built of gopher wood, and if it had to sit in water for any length of time, it had to be a type of wood that would not rot. God knew all of those details. The biblical word for an ark is "tebah." This is what was used for Noah's ark and the container that Moses was hidden in among the bulrushes. I doubt Noah had any control on what direction the vessel moved; he was at the very mercy of God.

He started from scratch, but ended up building something he did not have the capacity for or understand. God uses the most unlikely people, and often He will tell you to do something you have no reference or experience to do. Ours is to trust and obey what He says.

Determine not to be a slave of what other people want. The problem with putting more confidence in people than in God is you stop trusting your own judgment because you assume that other people will always know better than you. It is liberating to live life on God's terms and not on other people's' terms, because only God is perfect—people are flawed. Sometimes we just need to decide to stay away from people that insult our intelligence. Ultimately, the life we live and the dreams we fulfill are ours. God gives them to us, and we are responsible for their manifestation.

PART 4
A TAINTED IMAGE

CHAPTER NINE
INJURED BY EXPERIENCES

'"For my thoughts are not your thoughts,
neither are your ways,'
saith the LORD.
'For as the heavens are higher than the earth,
so are my ways higher than your ways,
and my thoughts than your thoughts'"
(Isaiah 55:8-9).

There is a relationship between your work and your world. Painful experiences or lack of a healthy family experience can be traumatizing. When someone has been damaged they often view God as unreliable, abusive, distant, demanding, emotionally detached and bound to abandon and ignore them. According to Dale and Juanita Ryan in *Distorted Images of God: Restoring Our Vision* (Ryan, Dale 2012), often our images of God influence us in a more powerful way than our ideas or formal convictions about God do.

A Change in Color

The Taj Mahal is famous for its craftsmanship, aesthetic balance, its story and various believes surrounding it. I wanted to focus on the fact that the Taj Mahal changes color from dusk to dawn because of the reflection of the sun on its white marble surface. At sunrise it is a pearly gray and pale pink, at noon it is a dazzling white and at sunset it appears to be an orange bronze, and at evening it becomes a translucent blue. A total of 28 types of precious and semi precious jewels were set in its marble when it was built. The turquoise was from Tibet, Jade from China, heavy white marble from Rajasthan. Age and pollution have however taken a toll on the Taj Mahal's marble as it is turning a brownish yellow. Burned fuel and garbage are causing its color to appear brownish yellow; and the pollution leaves particles that over time have changed its original white marble color.

Like the Taj Mahal, that goes through different seasons, stages and changes of color throughout the day (from dusk until dawn), a life once full of energy and breathtaking beauty can be affected by a toxic environment. Circumstances can damage the beauty God deposited, and can cause one's original color to change. The pollution of people's opinions, criticisms, emotional and psychological trauma, rejection, abuse, and neglect can be harmful; and like the Taj Mahal, the white marble can become a brownish yellow.

Local Indian women give the Taj Mahal a spa day, a mudpack facial is applied over the marble and washed off with brushes and the dirt vanishes and its glow is restored. Negative experiences can injure, damage and cause our color to change, but like those Indian women who give the Taj Mahal a spa day, the Holy Spirit is a present help in time of need Who can give you and I that necessary spa day to help restore the beauty God intended for you and I to display.

The Medicine of Life

I grew up in a broken home that eventually culminated in divorce. The experiences did a whole lot more harm than good to my perspective of God. Life can sometimes cripple your potential. For many years, I was very fearful of trying anything God asked me to do. It has taken years for me to gather the courage to write this book because I was so fearful to talk about a subject I love so much. I was convinced that if

I tried anything, God would disapprove and punish me when I failed, so I did not bother to try.

By His grace I am learning that what happens to me is not a direct measure of my worth or competence and that the enemy tried to rewire and damage what God intended and purposed for my life and destiny. My worth is not connected to my gifts, accomplishments and capabilities, but it is connected to God. Sometimes in life, we take the worst tasting medicine that we ingest through experiences and disappointments we don't understand. But as bad as the medicine may taste, it might just be what the patient needs to get better.

My pursuit for overcompensation can drive me in the opposite direction of my pursuit for God and discovering my image in Him. This happens because I become so caught up in a pursuit for an image for myself, instead of God's purpose. Pursuit of an image that is not the Image of God can:

- Paralyze our potential
- Prematurely abort dreams
- Contaminate my relationship with God and others
- Erode my ministry

Gideon is a great example of a man who doubted God; his face probably lost all color, as it flooded with disbelief and his heart pounded like it was about to escape in any minute from his rib cage.

Scriptures says,

"The angel of the LORD appeared to him and said to him,
'The LORD is with you, O valiant warrior.'
Then Gideon said to him,
'O my lord, if the LORD is with us,
why then has all this happened to us?
And where are all His miracles,
which our fathers told us about, saying,
'Did not the LORD bring us up from Egypt?'
But now the LORD has abandoned us and given us into the
hand of Midian.'

The LORD looked at him and said,
'Go in this your strength and deliver Israel
from the hand of Midian. Have I not sent you?'
He said to Him, 'O Lord, how shall I deliver Israel?
Behold, my family is the least in Manasseh,
and I am the youngest in my father's house?'
But the LORD said to him,
'Surely I will be with you,
and you shall defeat the Midians as one man'"
(Judges 6:12–16).

I can so picture Gideon looking around a little horrified and confused, thinking "valiant who!?!" Then God tells Him that he was to deliver the nation of Israel! Gideon must have been like, "Look God, I think you have the wrong guy. You must be confusing me with somebody else! Do you know who I am and can I just remind you of what I don't have!" Gideon saw who he was, the family he came from, what he didn't have and decided that disqualified him. God knew this about Gideon. That is why in Judges 7, God says in verse 9-15,

"Now the same night it came about that the Lord said to him,
'Arise, go down against the camp, for I have given it into
your hands. But if you are afraid to go down, go with Purah
your servant down to the camp, and you will hear what they
say; and afterward your hands will be strengthened that you
may go down against the camp.'
So he went with Purah his servant down to the outposts
of the army that was in the camp. Now the Midianites and
the Amalekites and all the sons of the east were lying in the
valley as numerous as locusts; and their camels were without
number, as numerous as the sand on the seashore.
When Gideon came, behold, a man was relating a dream
to his friend. And he said, 'Behold, I had a dream; a loaf
of barley bread was tumbling into the camp of Midian, and
it came to the tent and struck it so that it fell, and turned
it upside down so that the tent lay flat.'

His friend replied, 'This is nothing less than the sword of Gideon the son of Joash, a man of Israel; God has given Midian and all the camp into his hand.'

When Gideon heard the account of the dream and its interpretation, he bowed in worship. He returned to the camp of Israel and said, 'Arise, for the Lord has given the camp of Midian into your hands.'"

God knew that Gideon was afraid. This is why He orchestrated that the Midianite man have the dream about Gideon. God is so creative. I loved how He used a man Gideon did not even know. God used the foolishness of a dream to encourage Gideon, but to also let the Midianites know that He was the defender of Israel. The account of the cake of barley bread was so ridiculous, but also very special because God used the foolishness of bread eaten by the Israelites in their days of oppression to foretell the future of the Midianites. God knew that Gideon and the Israelites were probably injured by all the slavery and bondage they had been through, so much so that if He just told them He was going to fight for them, they would not believe it because of the injuries from their past experiences.

The Barley bread and cakes were considered to be poor folks' food and that is what God used to sustain the Israelites. It was ironically amusing that God later uses a giant barley cake as a symbol in a dream to remind Gideon that the Word of God would cause Gideon to be victorious over the Midianites. The sword of Gideon in this battle was the sword of the Word of God (Ephesians 6:17).

I looked up another account in the Bible involving this barley bread. Jesus in the New Testament fed the 5,000 in John 6 with barley bread that a little boy had. Jesus multiplied 5 loaves and 2 fish. The number 5 being the number of grace, which Jesus multiplied. I saw a connection between the 5 loaves of barley bread and the 5 books of the Mosaic law. The multiplying of the 5 loaves may have been symbolic of the multiplying of the 5 books of the Mosaic law. Jesus took the law and His grace multiplied and broke it down. What He did with that barley bread represented something much bigger, and more nourishing than what had been in the law. We have a greater grace that has been extended to us, even for our visions, hopes, desires and dreams.

I think what really ministered to me was the fact that Gideon was injured by his experiences, but God's strength was perfected in his weakness. You and I may look at what we have today, the little portion of "barley bread" that we have been living on, but God can use even that to crush your enemies. It is only in our little that His fullness is manifested and multiplied. The thing that may seem insignificant may be the thing God will use to bring your enemies to nothing, like that giant cake of barley bread.

I remember when God called me to be a Pastor. In all honesty, I rolled on the floor with laughter. I never saw myself as a minister, and like Gideon, I went straight to my family file. I am sure many of us know God has a sense of humor and often leads us to places we never dreamed or imagined. I could not receive what God was saying because of a poor perspective. A poor perspective of self can damage what we think, what we desire, and what we say. I am purposing to remind myself frequently that I am a whole person and enough, because of the price Jesus Christ paid for me. It is difficult to see His image while we are holding onto the masses of baggage of what people think and what we think of ourselves. The things others demonstrate to us can be a hindrance or the wrong thing.

He Took Him Outside

God will always throw something at you that will outlast you. God's ideas are bigger than ours. I love the story about how God called Abraham, and the encounter he had with God when God promised him that his descendants would be as numerous as the stars. Abraham was injured by the fact that he and his wife Sarah were childless. They had to deal with years of rejection and many years of failed attempts. In Genesis 15:5 it says, "And He took him outside and said, 'Now look toward the heavens, and count the stars, if you are able to count them.' And He said to him, 'So shall your descendants be.'"

What struck a chord in my spirit was that God took Abraham OUTSIDE. He could have told Abraham about his descendants being as numerous as the stars in the tent, but God took Abraham OUTSIDE. Abraham could not stay inside his tent (mindset), there was no room for what God wanted to say and do in the tent, and no room for God in his little tent. If Abraham had stayed in his little tent, he would have only believed God to the level of the roof of his tent; instead of the level of the expanse of the entire sky and galaxy.

Sometimes it takes God taking you outside the tent of your thinking, your own limitations for you to see. It takes a coming out—out of what you know, what you are used to, what happened to you, what you are comfortable with, what you can manage, what confines you, what you don't have, and what you understand. You have to come out of the security of the little or abundance that you think you have and out of your rationality, so you can see the promise God has for you.

Looking toward Heaven and seeing those stars was not just an experience God wanted so Abraham could see the numerical quantity of his blessing. It was a sign of a deposit God was making in his legacy. It was a royal status and a leadership quality God wanted to bestow on him, so he could see how his (Abraham's) descendants would rank in the earth ... as a "royal priesthood." Abraham was content with the blessing of having a son in his tent, but God wanted to give him a blessing beyond himself of a multitude of descendants as numerous as the stars in the sky.

C. S. Lewis once said, "You thought you were being made into a decent little cottage: but He is building a palace He intends to come and live in Himself."

On a Personal Note

Several years ago, I entered a video contest. I saw the poster by accident at school. I am not a fan of notice boards, but something drew me to this one. It was an ad about a video contest where the winners would win a monetary prize. I saw the deadline date to submit was the following day at 5 p.m. I called one of my friends who knew nothing about video and asked them to help record the video. I came up with a few last minute creative ideas and recorded the video using my laptop and phone! (I knew a little about video editing so that was a plus). We shot the video; I spent all night editing it and finished around 5 a.m. the next morning, just in time to get ready for 7 a.m. class. I submitted the video with the hopes of winning the monetary prize. I was just thinking, "If I can win the money, I could buy books and other things for next semester for school."

Three days after my submission, I realized the competition I entered was a national contest; I guess I missed the fine print. I felt intimidated, afraid and was convinced I would not win. However, I was wrong. I was one of three winners selected and the video contest ended up sending me on a trip to California as a student delegate at a conference for 3,000+ educators. I attended, representing the 50,000+ student body at my school. On the last day of the conference, I was set on going to Disneyland with other students, and at that point, not even wild horses could drag me out of a Disneyland adventure!

However, through a series of events, one of the organizers of the conference decided she wanted to add an African female student to the panel for the session they were having that afternoon (mind you, during my Disneyland time).

I tried to worm my way out of the panel, and the lady didn't know me and had never heard me speak, but she pleaded and pleaded with me. So that afternoon I was "the sacrificial African lamb" that missed the Disneyland appointment. I had no idea that the panel was about two hours long, and I had to come up with 25 minutes of sense to talk about educational experiences, goals and my educational concerns as a foreign student. I had never said anything in front of 3,000+ people with video cameras and photographers' cameras going off.

Anyone who knows me will tell you I am a severe introvert. I was nervous and could feel a sea of eyes staring at me. While I was speaking, I did not realize God had set me up. There was somebody sitting in the audience who was intrigued by what I said, so much so that after the session they came and introduced themselves to me. They handed me a business card, asked for my contact information and walked off. I had no idea who they were.

The Chancellor of my school happened to be in the panel session and heard that I was the sacrificial lamb that had missed out on Disneyland for the panel. She arranged for me to go there after the session and paid for everything. I was grateful I got my Disney experience, and a few days after recovering from the conference festivities, I received a call from the person who had given me their card. They were calling to let me know that they had sent my video and recommended me to a University that wanted to give me a scholarship, even before interviewing me or seeing my grades! To cut a long story short I went to this school and graduated with an education worth $180,000.

The point of my story is that you never know what you are attempting and what other doors God will open. "What may seem to be a small door may have a big door behind it" (Bishop Tudor Bismark). My perspective was poor and limited to the monetary prize, but I had no idea that there was another blessing and door attached to what I could see because God always sees further than what I can afford. The lesson I learned from this experience was that there are things that will never happen in my life if I don't take that step of faith and just try. "My gift made room for me through this experience" (Proverbs 18:16).

Creativity Crushers and Roadblocks

Our creativity can have several roadblocks and things that crush our potential including:

1. Not realizing we have the capacity to create.

The biggest deterrent to people expressing any creativity they may have is not realizing that we all have the capacity to create. Creativity has been reduced to being an artist, designer, musician and writer. However, it is who we all are and a quality we all have been given, and a need we all have to fulfill for our lives and the lives of those around us to be meaningful. An estimated 3 out of 4 people (75%) don't think they are creative (Morrison, Mary Kay, 2012). I don't know about you, but that statistic really bothers me because those statistics translate to the number of ideas we are losing or miss out on experiencing every day.

2. Creating in a world of evaluation – Self and Other's Evaluation

The creative process involves being able to create forward and keep on moving along in spite of blockages and roadblocks. It takes visualization and sorting through a mess of ideas to find ones that actually work. We all need to break through some things to receive a breakthrough. Living in a world where we are measured by others by culture, evaluation can affect what and how we create. Evaluating too soon can lead to prematurely aborting God ideas we may have. A writing rampage where you jot down everything helps until you literally run out of steam, and then go away and leave the ideas for a few days, come back after prayer and revisit and evaluate what you wrote. The danger with self-evaluation is because we do not fully know what God put on the inside of us. That evaluation is not based on what God said or did, but on what we think of ourselves or what others have said.

3. Doing what people said versus doing what God said.

In my personal life, this stemmed from a poor image of God, a poor self-image, and having poor boundaries. Sometimes we have too many boundaries, very few boundaries, or no boundaries at all. I had none, and often allowed people to tell me who I was, and what they felt God wanted me to have. I came to a point where out of frustration I woke up one day and decided to take responsibility for the outcome of my life. People must earn the right to hear what God is depositing in my heart. It must not come easy and it must not come free. What God is releasing is not for everyone to hear, even if they are my brother or sister in Christ.

God makes a deposit and nobody besides the Holy Spirit can see it. He may choose to reveal a glimpse of that deposit to someone, but as the Word says, no eye has seen and no ear has head, neither has it entered into the heart of man what God has prepared for those that love Him. (1 Corinthians 2:9). People will always reduce your ideas to what they know, what they don't know, and what they think about you.

4. Fear

I talked about this earlier in the book, but I can't say this enough. Some people fear failure and others are fearful of success. Avoiding failure means that you will be avoiding the breakthrough and success of an idea. A breakthrough can only take place when you break through something. The seed of an idea/creativity can flourish in the soil of failure. Good soil is full of all sorts of nasty things, bacteria, fungi, worms and insects, but the more life soil contains, the more nutrients it has (Crouse, David, 2015). Sometimes the more failed attempts and difficult experiences we have, the more opportunities we have to grow and learn and develop mature creative ideas. There are countless stories from the lives of leaders, billionaires, entrepreneurs, film directors, presidents, parents, animators, scientists, writers, athletes, musicians, and business people, etc., whose lives and success were shaped in the "soil of their failures."

5. It should all be clear and make perfect sense.

There is nothing about creating, innovation or life that is neat and tidy. God created life out of darkness and some without form and void. We are not called into order, but to create order out of chaos. When everything is neat and tidy there is a level of comfort that comes because everything is safely tucked away in a clean and put together space. I love comfort, but comfort is always an enemy to our ability to take risks. (Dan Stevens) Director of "The Terminator," James Cameron, was living out of his car when he was writing "The Terminator." He could barely make two ends meet, but he persevered and sold the rights to his screenplay for $1 (was still able to direct the film, and it went on to make $77 million). Cameron did not create out of comfort.

Daniel Craig, (James Bond), also slept on park benches in London early in his acting career, but went on to become James Bond, who gained much acclaim for his role in the movie. Neither of these people's circumstances were "ideal" for creativity, but still they pursued their dreams and took great risks.

6. Poor image of self

We must be confident of this one thing, "that He who began a good work in you will bring it to completion unto the day of Jesus Christ" (Philippians 1:6). I have this confidence, that God released the idea, and He will carry me through to the fulfillment and manifestation of the idea.

Self-limitations we have to deal with are often self-imposed. I hear what I say to myself everyday more than I hear what everyone around me has said or is saying. We sometimes develop negative thought patterns in our childhood, and we have to unlearn them because our brains are wired for responding to situations via a pattern. Nurturing pain and negative self-talk is something that needs rewiring, so we can nurture our spirits, intellect, relationships, finances, health, work, and emotions with the Word of God.

7. Have a mindset that tries.

Today is definitely a great day to start acting like the person you have always wanted to be (Robin Sharma). Focus on what you can do, rather than what you failed to do. Measuring our failures to successes confuses the whole process, because failure cannot be measured against success, failure is necessary to success. Thomas Edison should be our go-to-story whenever we are tempted to quit; he tried to create the light bulb and failed 1,000 times!

8. Avoid people who dismiss the things God shows you.

When you spend more time listening to naysayers, you ignore what God has put in your heart. Jesus had many naysayers, but He never allowed what they said to define Who He was or what He did. Jesus came and preached the Kingdom, an idea that raised a whole lot more than just eyebrows. Everything Jesus said challenged culture, tradition and mindsets that had been in place for generations. Listening to naysayers will only take us as far as what they said. So, if they said, "You can't do it," and you listen to them, you won't do it.

9. Analysis paralysis

The leprosy of the analysis paralysis battle is real. In overanalyzing, I sometimes don't end up doing anything because I tend to anticipate failure even before trying. Who I am is not attached to failure; failure is just a part of the process. I had my fair share of analysis paralysis during the birthing of this book. I am a very deep thinker. When I see a pencil,

I don't just see a pencil. I wonder which tree was cut down so I could use this pencil, where the tree was, and how many people in the world have ever used the brand of pencil I am.

Over thinking can cause us to not do anything. Feeding our minds with information is like watering a garden. If you flood a garden with too much water, the roots will rot and be stunted—no new growth will take place. There will be a lack of oxygen, and the soil will appear green. Too much information can have a similar effect and cause more harm than good. Water like information is a good thing, but too much of it can end up working against us.

10. Speed kills creativity.

We need to allow ideas to fully mature and that takes time, and oftentimes, a considerable amount of time. If you are anything like me, patience is an issue for me. We live in a culture of convenience, where everything is instant and drive through. Even dreams and ideas are fulfilled in the drive through process. The culture of convenience is such a huge problem that convenience has even started to creep into the Church. People want triumph without process, but sometimes God will lengthen the creative process so you have the capacity to stand and stay where God wants you. I often imagine something, and then I am ready to make it happen within hours because the vision or idea I would have seen is so real to me. But sometimes we have to submit an idea or the process to God for a time when God will use it. He knows when we are ready.

In what we do with the totality of our lives, we will be able to tell the most about who we are and what our priorities were. Exhaustion also hurts creativity. Busyness can hinder creativity because our time becomes so consumed with the wrong things that there is very little or no time left for the right things. A battle between obligation and purpose takes place, and often with responsibility, it is hard to choose purpose. Sometimes busyness comes from a lack of direction. When we have clear goals and details about how those goals will be accomplished, we avoid anything that would steal the time we could dedicate to making that goal a reality.

Come to life

"This world is a great sculptor's shop. We are statues and there's a rumor going around in the shop that some of us are someday going to come to life." (C. S. Lewis). There are people who need to come to life, and decide to stop living like a lifeless sculptor. Some people have a lack of achievement mindset and others have an over achievement mindset, but it takes making a right achievement focused mindset to stay focused and not be busy with all the wrong things. Having a relationship with the Holy Spirit helps us because He helps us in our weakness and He lovingly points out those things to us that we need to change.

Relationships that Injure

Mark Ambrose once said, "Show me your friends, and I'll show you your future." An easy way to conform is in the company we keep. Time and relationships are important to our lives; so important that it is necessary to reject anything and anyone who does not help you become the best you. I love what Warren Buffet said when he was asked what was one of the best choices he had made in his life that helped him become a billionaire. His response was, "The best thing I did was choose the right heroes." There are times I have been stuck in the same place because I made the poor choice of surrounding myself with friends who hated to work and had no desire to improve themselves. I later sat down one day and wrote down a list with three columns,

- A column for people who were improving my life
- A column for people keeping me in the same place

- A column for people who were dragging me down

I compared each column. I was a little shocked by the result, so much that I had to ask God to show me what I needed to change. After all, the quickest way to find honey is to follow those who are bees (Matshona Dhliwayo).

Eagles or Vultures

I wanted to throw in some interesting comparisons between eagles and vultures I gathered from National Geographic ...

Vultures

I am not a personal fan of vultures. I know God made them for a purpose and that they are like nature's garbage collectors that get rid of the mess—a valuable role in the ecosystem. I think what bothers me about them is that they are content with eating leftover dead things that would otherwise rot. Some people I have met are content with meditating and living with and on dead things. Dead things represent the past. Vultures scavenge and steal other animal's prey; they don't hunt for their own. It is not okay to be content with doing nothing authentic, challenging or fulfilling, because that is what we were created for.

Vultures, if I can be honest, are ugly birds, with their bold, featherless heads, and bloated creepy and clumsy looking appearance. I was surprised to read about how they fly often at the mercy of currents, don't flap much and often they wait for opportunities to feed on another animal's prey, rather than seeking out their own prey and opportunities. The fact that they feed on whatever carcasses they can find, defenseless animals like newborns and the wounded, shows me that they are unable to control their own destiny and that they hate to work for food. Vultures depend primarily on luck and often eat until they are so full they can't fly. I think it's safe to say, vultures are lazy birds; they risk nothing, fight for nothing and everything they eat is already dead when they find it.

Eagles

Eagles keep their eyes on their vision no matter what. Eagles are monogamous; they have a strong mate fidelity and sight fidelity. Eagles focus and can keep their eyes on something as far as 5 km/2 miles away from the air; they keep focus so much that no obstacle will remove them or distract them from focusing on the prey until they grab it. Eagles don't eat dead things. Many other birds will hide or seek shelter whenever there is a storm, but eagles love storms, and relish challenges because they can cause them to rise and fly higher to new levels. Eagles test before they trust. It's important to test people no matter how well meaning they appear before you trust them with your ideas.

Eagles are attractive, confident, well-groomed and good-looking birds. They work for everything they eat. Eagles often fly alone, but will get around other eagles, if there is a common goal, to eat. They don't mix with other birds, just eagles, and they are bold and decisive. Eagles also tend not to remain in the same place for a long time, and they don't have a problem shedding off old habits. At this point, if you read these two descriptions and are thinking hmm ... someone I know is just like this ... PRAY and ask God for wisdom on what to do about that relationship ...

**"Keep away from people who try to
Belittle your ambitions. Small people
Always do that, but the really great make you
feel that you too can become great"
– Mark Twain**

CHAPTER TEN

YARDSTICK SYNDROME

"When they returned from spying out the land,
at the end of forty days,
they proceeded to come to Moses and Aaron
and to all the congregation of the sons of Israel
in the wilderness of Paran, at Kadesh;
and they brought back word to them
and to the entire congregation and showed them
the fruit of the land. Thus they told him, and said,
'We went into the land where you sent us;
and it certainly does flow with milk and honey,
and this is its fruit.
Nevertheless, the people who live in the land are strong,
and the cities are fortified and very large;
and moreover, we saw the descendants of Anak there'"
(Numbers 13:25-28).

Giants or Grapes

The spies went to look at the land, and they saw it did flow with milk and honey, but they also saw "the people." God shows us something we have, or can accomplish. We see it, but then we see what we don't have, and we see "people."

I tried to imagine the whole scene. The spies did not come with photographs, but with tangible evidence of what God said. They saw the clusters of grapes that were so big they had to be carried between two men on a pole! God's intent was for them to see their promise, and to bring back the report of the Lord. In Numbers 13:1, 2, we read that a man was sent from each tribe so they could testify. God sent them to explore that land which He was giving them.

There is always a giant that will try and keep you from the promise, but the promise land was already a done deal with God. The giants they were seeing were just occupying it for the Israelites until they came to claim it. Sometimes the giants you see are only there because they are just occupying your blessing for you. It is amazing how many of us are so afraid to even touch the dreams that God gives us. Sometimes it is easier to long to return to the bondage than to believe for the word of blessing from God. It's almost like our sinful nature has tendencies to relapse back into sin and despair, even after seeing demonstrations of God's power.

The devil will always use doubt to dissuade you and cause you to withdraw from pursuing His promises and blessings. Some of us see ourselves way smaller than how even our enemies see us. What we believe about ourselves significantly can affect what we become. I found myself asking myself this question, "What occupies your thoughts? The grapes or the giants?" Grapes represent the fruitfulness, promises, provisions of God, and the Giants represent the lies the enemy uses to frustrate and steal the promises of God over our lives.

Grapes were the first things to be planted after the flood. Grapes were also a symbol in Jewish history of Yahweh's promise about the Promise Land. If your motivation and focus is the grapes, then the giants won't even matter. Once you have tasted grapes, giants don't matter because you realize that giants are not there to control your promise. Giants are what you have to deal with to get your grapes (promise). Decide whether you will spend your life measuring your giants, or weighing and gathering your grapes.

Comparison

We live in a society that puts heavy importance on

competition, and that we can never be content until we have everything that other people have. Competition is not a bad thing, but when it becomes the main thing, we lose sight of God's purpose. God gave us a creative ability, not so we could fully express how much better we are than others, but so we could show how incredible and multifaceted He is.

Cain compared himself to Abel, and ended up killing his brother because he was consumed with jealousy. The disciples often compared themselves to each other. Comparisons prevent us from living by faith. We have similarities, not so we can compare ourselves to each other, but so we would not forget we didn't make ourselves, but came from God. Comparison is like accepting a lie in place of a truth. There are many platforms on social media that make it easy for us to compare ourselves to others. People post images of their accomplishments and "perfect" lives. We hardly see any posts about anxieties, laziness, weaknesses, insecurities or failures.

We will never live above the way we see God and the way we see ourselves. Some find hurting or punishing themselves as a way to protect themselves from facing the reality of not being able to meet the expectation of what they cannot be to those who make unreasonable demands on them. Self-loathing is not a respecter of anyone and makes no exemptions; it even afflicts those who seem to have everything. Jesus said,

> *"... Why do you call Me good?*
> *No one is good but One, that is, God ..."*
> (Matthew 19:17).

Mephibosheth is great example of a character in the Bible who loathed himself. Self-loathing is to experience a strong sense of disgust or dislike with oneself. It is an intense aversion of self. (Merriam Webster). Scripture says,

> *"Now Jonathan, Saul's son,*
> *had a son crippled in his feet.*
> *He was five years old when the report of Saul*

and Jonathan came from Jezreel,
and his nurse took him up and fled.
And it happened that in her hurry to flee,
he fell and became lame.
And his name was Mephibosheth"
(2 Samuel 4:4).

"Mephibosheth, the son of Jonathan the son of Saul,
came to David and fell on his face and prostrated himself.
And David said, 'Mephibosheth.'
And he said, 'Here is your servant!'
David said to him, 'Do not fear,
for I will surely show kindness to you
for the sake of your father Jonathan,
and will restore to you all the land of your grandfather Saul;
and you shall eat at my table regularly.'
Again he prostrated himself and said,
'What is your servant,
that you should regard a dead dog like me?'"
(2 Samuel 9:6-8).

Mephibosheth's crippling was due to the circumstances of life; it was not his fault he was dropped. He reduced himself to "a dead dog" and could not imagine that anyone could love him. He had already decided that God did not see him anymore because of what happened to him. How many of us are like Mephibosheth? Were we dropped one way or another? Did we get dropped from the team, fail an exam, get dropped by a boyfriend or girlfriend, apply for the business loan to every bank in our city and get denied? Did we get fired or laid off from a job, did not get picked by the pastor for the leadership team, were left out of an important family event, or our family never believed in us? At some point in our lives, we have gotten dropped by someone. Mephibosheth's condition was like many of our conditions when we come to Christ, helpless and fearful.

Being dropped doesn't mean you are a failure. One only

become a failure when they believe and start to act like one. There are many people who have been through very traumatic experiences and very painful circumstances. Christians are not immune to self-hatred, and because we sometimes put more pressure on ourselves to perform, when we don't measure up, we are deeply disappointed. We hate ourselves for how we look, what we have done and not done, what has happened to us, and what we are failing to accomplish in life. Self-loathing disagrees with what God says about us. God said He made us in His image—He looked at what He had made and said, "This is very good."

Self-loathing is detrimental to our creative process, and it comes from a misunderstanding of the magnitude of God's grace. God pours daily on us His:

- Provisional grace – James 1:17
- Saving grace – Ephesians 2:8
- Sanctifying grace – Philippians 1:6
- Common grace – Matthew 5:45
- Sustaining grace – 2 Corinthians 12:9
- Serving grace – 1 Peter 4:10

Self-loathing has its roots in childhood or in a bad experience. (Stacey Freedenthal, 2017). People tend to manifest their experiences as they get older. Some of us start on the right foot like Mephibosheth—everything is going well until someone drops us. Self-loathing also stems from how our parents or primary caregivers viewed themselves. We know very little about how Jonathan viewed himself, but Saul was Mephibosheth's grandfather. From the time that Saul had an encounter with the Prophet Samuel, when Samuel anointed him, we know that he suffered from a sense of inferiority. He was self-conscious of the tribe he came from, "a Benjaminite, from the least of the tribes of Israel."

Mephibosheth is not the only one. Jeremiah was called by God, but presented God with excuses. Jeremiah viewed himself through the lenses of his shortcomings. Scripture says,

"Then I said, 'Alas, Lord GOD!
Behold, I do not know how to speak,
because I am a youth.'
But the LORD said to me,
'Do not say, 'I am a youth,'
because everywhere I send you, you shall go,
And all that I command you, you shall speak.
'Do not be afraid of them,
For I am with you to deliver you,' declares the LORD"
(Jeremiah 1:6-8).

He reminded God that he could not speak, and that he was a youth. God brought things into perspective to correct Jeremiah, "Do not say I am a youth." To God youth or old age cannot confine or hinder His purpose. God sent Jeremiah, and because He sent him, He would be responsible for what Jeremiah would have to say. God makes no mistakes.

Self-loathing and self-doubt can cripple potential and cause us to drift away from God. Short-circuited love can affect how we view God, others, and God's assignment for our lives. Loving ourselves is not possible unless we first love God, because we are His, we learn love from Him and who we are can only be found in Him.

CHAPTER ELEVEN
CREATIVE CALL
FOR WOMEN

"Charm is deceitful and beauty is passing,
But a woman who fears the Lord
she shall be praised."
(Proverbs 31:30)

"A woman's place before anything else, is in God."
- Dr. Myles Munroe

Women have the potential to be champions of innovation and empowerment because they are social by nature, and know how to connect with other women. Every woman can experience the life that God intended for her, if she can remember that the place where she starts out is in God.

I wanted to include a chapter on women and creativity, because as a woman I know how challenging it is for some women to express their creative ideas. My hope is not to put off my brothers, but that you would learn something about the women you love. There are many things I could talk about, but I decided to focus on a few areas where women's conditions make it difficult for them to be innovative and creative.

A Woman's Potential

Women face harder choices between professional and social success and personal fulfillment in many parts of the world (Sheryl Sandberg). Women are held back from fulfilling their God-given potential, and are often abused or even seen as deserving abuse. Many women tend to be misunderstood by those who should love and protect them. In the Third World, women are still politically and economically oppressed.

The enemy hates women, and he works overtime to try and shut down the hearts of many women. In shutting her heart, he knows he can shut down her purpose, her family, her community and her nation, and everything else in her life. Satan assaults the identities of women daily, because he wants to control how women live, so they live below their God-given potential. The enemy tries to keep women in bondage because he fears what God has put in them.

The statistics are shocking about how many women are still living in some form of modern day oppression. Men seem more active in shaping ideas about Africa. Many factors prevent gifted women from pursuing creative careers. Sadly, not enough spot-light is put on women's achievements. In Africa, women face abject poverty, in the Middle East, women are deprived of basic human rights, in America and Europe, women are forced to juggle careers and family, often in a single parent home. A third of women in developing countries are still excluded from decision-making on household purchases, are treated like minors in the Arab world, and one in ten women have no say on how their own earnings are spent. Almost two thirds of illiterate adults in the world are women—from Northern Africa, sub-Sahara Africa and Southern Asia.

The challenge a majority of women in the Third World face is not having the luxury to create. It is difficult to create when you cannot meet your basic needs. It is easy to have no mental energy after spending the entire day working. Lack of economic independence can also drain the creative process and abilities of women. Women also earn less and have less access to programming and funding.

Time Poverty

One of the biggest enemies to a woman's ability to

think creatively and do something meaningful is a lack of time. Women live under a variety of circumstances with varying degrees of challenges around the world. Some Women in Africa struggle with "time poverty" because in Africa, women's time does not belong to them. From the time they are young girls, they spend thousands of hours, more than boys, doing unpaid work because the African society puts more responsibility on girls. (Merelli, Annalisa, 2016).

Many women also don't have the time to attend school, be with their families and run businesses in the midst of all the other responsibilities they have, especially in poor countries. Women are robbed of opportunities and potential because of the social issues where women are expected to devote more time to sweeping, scrubbing, nursing and caring for children.

Globally, women spend an average of 4.5 hours doing unpaid work (Miller, Claire Cain, 2016). According to studies by Practical Action, women in India spend 374 hours every year collecting firewood—having a stove and electricity could save them a lot of time. Eighty-five percent of daily energy in villages in Africa is spent on fetching water, and it is estimated that women in developing countries in Africa have the potential to add trillions of dollars to the annual GDP of their nation through agriculture, joining the workforce, community projects and running small business.

The problem with time poverty is it leaves millions of women deprived of the opportunities that God intended for them to have. A woman in the Arab world for example, juggles far more responsibilities than their male counterparts. There is a misconception that, "Sons and not daughters should be professionally motivated" (Leila Hoteit) in the Arab world. The experiences of women in the western world also are different from the experiences of women in the Arab world, the East and Africa. Women do two thirds of the labor, and own less than one percent of the world's assets in developing countries. Imagine if those millions of women were able to receive the help they needed how that would change their outlook on life, and their opportunities then create something that would make a difference in their families, communities, and their nations.

Women who are uneducated are also the most vulnerable and marginalized. Girls make up 53% of all children out of primary school and 52% of all adolescents out of lower secondary school. (Reference – GLOBAL PARTNERSHIP FOR EDUCATION). By giving women in these poverty cycles access to information, education, proper sanitation (running water and electricity), healthcare and technology, much time and energy can be saved, enabling women to have time to grow and become enterprising.

Women are hindered in many ways in the developing world. (UNESCO report, 2014).

- A main one is limited capital
- Inward thinking from the national leadership
- Social norms
- Gender stereotypes
- Sexual harassment
- Low confidence
- Social stigma
- Lack of skills and role models

Challenges that Affect our Ability to Create

Some women have a storm going on inside of them. Women tend to not shake off rejection as quickly as men do. As women, often times we are completely unaware of the incessant chatter that goes on in our heads. It is important to be conscious of the thoughts we have and the way we think, because behind every action is a thought, and our fruit is not in our thoughts it is in our actions.

The struggle we have is that much of our creative energy ends up being drained by the struggles and all the other responsibilities we have. Social expectations affect women's abilities to be innovative, particularly in developing countries.

There are often women who won't try anything because of fear of being labeled aggressive. Women who have great ideas often have similar concerns, that there aren't enough mentors out there in their field who are women.

I can testify that when I was writing this book, all of the people with the exception of one woman, who gave information on writing and publishing this book, were men. Balancing business and family can be a challenge for women, too. In developing countries, women have to deal with a lack of education and resources, and there are often role conflicts in marriages. Most of the battles women wage, are battles of the past. Often some women are defined by what is behind them, instead of what is in front of them.

Women struggle with:

- Heartache
- Disappointment
- Fear
- Insecurity
- Abandonment
- Shame
- Bitterness
- Rejection
- Unforgiveness
- Anger
- Regret
- Poor self-confidence

The sound of other people's opinions often plays over and over in my head. However, the opinions of others should never completely drown out my ability to hear from God. When God calls you to do something, always be prepared to be misunderstood. Women are also still put in boxes—a difficult box for us to get out of is the box we jump into ourselves by choice. The aspects of our lives that drain our creative juices everyday revolve around things we often have little or no control over.

God Made Eve

Women dream more for others than they do for themselves. It is important as a woman to reclaim your ability to dream. The journey is not easy, but certainly worth it. Men have no trouble finding an abundance of role models, and do not face the challenge to imagine that they can actually effect change. When you don't have a family to support your dreams and visions as a woman, it can be discouraging. When there are so many expectations on you, and people pulling at you for attention in all directions, it is not easy for some women to be their authentic self, but it is so important to own being you.

Society puts so much pressure on women. It paints a picture that it is more important to maintain your public journey, even at the expense of your private journey. I spent so many years being frustrated, trying to be somebody I was not. I have decided to never let anything or anyone define my potential or me ever again. Only God can and will define me.

It started with taking the limits off of myself. Limits like:

- I can't afford it
- I am way too old
- I don't have the time
- I never went to school
- It won't happen to me
- No one I know has ever done this before
- I have made too many mistakes in the past
- I am not creative

God made Eve, Adam did not make Eve

Adam was asleep when God created Eve. There are women who still look for a man to define who they are, what they can have and their worth, but it was not Adam that made Eve … it was God. The more women would realize this, the potential and dreams that would be birthed in women all over the world would be exciting. God is attracted to women who dream big, and women who are bold and willing to step out and try something they have never tried before. There are women all over the world who are realizing that they have the power to change or redefine the status quo.

Focusing on impact brings greater fulfillment and starting with a bigger objective can make a difference in other women's lives. Zakia Mohammadhi is a leader who has a local cycling team in Afghanistan. She is inspiring and teaching many Afghan women in the villages to ride bicycles to get around, if they don't have transportation to get to school. Having a bigger objective comes from paying attention to what really matters and seeing the value of who you are. You, too, have something to give that is valuable and can help others.

A Princess Redefined

I know different people have mixed feelings about Disney, but I wanted to focus on an idea they had earlier this year. Disney started a campaign that is shattering and redefining the image of what it means to be a Princess (Rowley, 2017). A princess used to wear pretty dresses, speak sweetly, and end up in dangerous situations where she needed to be rescued. Then, there was the prince of her dreams, ready to fight for her and make her dreams come true. The Disney #DreamBigPrincess campaign decided to end this stereotype of women, and presented a challenge to female photographers, who were asked to take photos of women dreaming big and share those photos to encourage women and girls.

The photos were shared on social media, and generated one million likes and shares in five days. Disney saw a need women and girls around the world had a need for more strong female role models. The problem with this picture of waiting for a prince to make your dreams come true is in thinking that someone else can come rescue you and make your dreams come true; when God has called you to fulfill a greater purpose that He has and wants to help you fulfill Himself.

Women in Innovation

Women are often unnamed and unacknowledged for their efforts and heroism in history. I believe we are in a season where women are rising up, and are realizing that they are not accessories or things to be used decoratively—they are leaders with purpose. God cares about women, and men depend on women in more ways than we all think about. It begins at birth where God uses a woman's womb to bring a child into the world. Many teachers around the world in schools who teach and nurture men and women are women. "A woman is like a teabag," you never know how strong she will be until she has been in hot water. (Eleanor Roosevelt). The potential of women is often not realized or is overlooked, until like that teabag, she has gone through a trying circumstance.

God loves women and desires to use women in innovation, too. God loves innovation, and His very nature is innovative. Innovation is incremental (Bezo); it is important to determine today to take that first step. "The more women innovate, the more they inspire and allow other women to innovate" (Fumbi Chima, 2016).

There are many inspiring stories of innovative women from around the world, but time will only give me chance to mention a few. Ciiru Waithaka from Kenya founder of FunKidz children's furniture company designs products inspired by African stories. The Rwanda Basket Company is also making an impact on the women in Rwanda. Hutu and Tutsi women come together to weave baskets and talk about their challenges. They are finding that they have many more similarities than they have differences. If you know anything about Rwanda's history and the war challenges between Hutu's and Tutsi's, this is a huge accomplishment and a beacon of hope for this community of women in Rwanda. (Amapour, 2008).

Malala Yousafzai, a Pakistani activist for female education, was shot by the Taliban because of her advocacy—she survived. She used an anonymous blog about her life under the Taliban and her writing impacted the education rights of Pakistani girls. She had a desire beyond herself. "I want every girl, every child to be educated." (BBC, 2014). Her campaign earned her the respect of many leaders around the world; her advocacy has become an international movement and was awarded a Nobel Peace Prize. She was born in 1997.

President Ellen Johnson Sirleaf is another notable lady who has given her life to serving the nation of Liberia. She is affectionately known as the "Iron Lady" and as a woman who has experienced much resistance to her pursuit for leadership in Liberia. President Sirleaf experienced a lot of rejection and persecution and went into exile, but she never lost the love and commitment she had for her country. She was sentenced to 10 years in prison when she spoke out, and today, she is the President. She is definitely a trailblazer and the first African female President. She is a great source of hope for women.

The first step is asking God to give you the courage to do it. God used many women in the Bible to redeem, rescue, protect, nurture, lead, intercede, carry His redemption plan, and stand in the gap. We are not just 'sugar and spice and everything nice,' but loaded with the power and presence of God.

I believe today is a perfect day to be living on the continent of Africa. The technological advancements and many changes create a critical time to be innovative and impact the stories told about our nations. I definitely want to contribute to the rebranding of the African continent as a trailblazer in creativity and innovation. Some of the dreams, goals and desires we pursue can create hope and inspiration for others. We never know who will be inspired by our courage and faith as women.

**"We need to remember that we are
All created creative and can
invent new scenarios,
as frequently as
they are needed."
- Maya Angelou**

PART 5
HIS
VISION
IMAGE

CHAPTER TWELVE
ACCORDING TO DESIGN

"But God has chosen the foolish things of the world
to put to shame the wise,
and God has chosen the weak things of the world
to put to shame the things which are mighty"
(1 Corinthians 1:27).

Every good work, simple, artistic, technical, huge, small, business related, people related, scientific, starts out as an idea. I tried to remember how many ideas I have had in the past. They are so many I have lost track and forgotten most of them. There are probably more creative ideas than there are people in the world, if we combined all the ideas every person has had. Ideas come with opportunities, relationships and blessings. Often when we dismiss an idea, we are dismissing the opportunity and blessing attached to that idea.

Creative for His Kingdom

God gives us ideas to further the work of His Kingdom. We are called by God to be fruitful and to multiply—so our creative ideas should be ideas that bear fruit and multiply. I spoke about Abraham in an earlier chapter. Abraham just wanted to be a father to a son, but God wanted to give him Isaac and make him a father of nations that were attached to his son. God wanted to give Abraham and Sarah a blessing that would not just flow to them, but one that would flow through them and touch many people's lives by making Abraham a father of nations.

God gives ideas for a purpose. They are not just random thoughts we have. Ideas serve as gifts in our lives, not just gifts for us, but for others. In Matthew 25:14-30, out of the servants who were given the talents, the one who went and buried his talent aborted an idea that God was trying to multiply through him. The talent he hid in the ground represented an idea God wanted him to use. God holds us accountable for the ideas He gives us. Every idea and resource He gives is to be used for the Kingdom of God. When God releases an idea (blessing), that idea has an expectation attached to it. The expectation God has is that we take that idea and use it to further His work and bless others.

Sometimes our inability to respond to God and the ideas He gives cannot only hinder our progress, but that of others. God uses the ideas He gives us to bless us and other people. Procrastination is an enemy to ideas and innovation, because it erodes our ideas, and we eventually cannot even remember what that idea was. When we procrastinate and do not pursue the ideas God gives or our passions, "Someone will hire you to help them pursue theirs." (Tony Gaskins). When we show God we can build His Kingdom we take the ideas He gives and put them to Kingdom use—then God will multiply them. When we choose to be faithful with a little, God will entrust much more to us.

The Power of Planning

Planning is an act of faith. It takes a great measure of faith to write down a plan. Faith is seeing the future and trusting God with that future, regardless of the circumstances. To exercise your faith you need a documented vision or plan. God honors and respects the time you take to make a plan. "Planning is the highest expression of your faith." (Dr. Myles Munroe). Ours is to obey and write down the plan that God lays on our hearts. God's responsibility is to fulfill or bring that plan to pass. The Message Bible says,

*"Long before He [God] laid down
earth's foundations,
He had us in mind, had settled on us as
the focus of His love,
to be made whole and holy by His love.
Long, long ago
He decided to adopt us into
His family through Jesus Christ.
(What pleasure He took in planning this!)
He wanted us to enter into the celebration
of His lavish gift-giving
by the handoff His beloved Son"* (Ephesians 1:3-6).

The devil plans disaster, mayhem and confusion, but God is the Master planner of our destiny.

Chosen by God

Nothing in creation is out of place. When I read about the account of Bezalel, the son of Uri being commissioned to build the Lord's temple, there is an important detail of the account I missed. In verses one and two it says, "Then the LORD said to Moses, 'See <u>I have chosen</u> Bezalel son of Uri, the son of Hur of the tribe of Judah.'" I want to focus on the part that says, see "<u>I have chosen</u>." This spoke volumes to me. God did not ask Moses to pick someone, or to make an announcement for any volunteers to step forward to do the work. God did not ask Moses to recommend anyone, or see if anyone knew someone who would be fit for the job.

It says God chose Bezalel. And that God put His Spirit in Bezalel. In Exodus 31:2-3, it says that God "filled him with the Spirit of God, with skill, ability and knowledge in all kinds of craft." God did not tell Bezalel to find information in books, or to attend design school (which is great to do to sharpen your craft). It says, "I have filled him." God chose who He wanted to gift with the ability to design the temple. God chooses our abilities and not us. Often we reject the gifts God has given us.

We will look for any opportunity to auction or trade them in for someone else's gift, but God chose what gifts we were to have by His design and Divine purpose. Everyone's gift is so much a part of who they are and who God called them to be.

I am so glad Jesus knew what His gift was and that He did not hoard it, waste it, reject it or hide it; otherwise, we would have all missed out on His gift of salvation and the redemption of our souls. It had me asking if there was any gift I was hiding that God gave me that could impact the lives of others?

When God was telling Moses that He had filled Bezalel with His Spirit, this was something God had already done before He told Moses to pick Bezalel. God already has us ready for what He has called us to do. He has predestined it, prearranged it and predetermined it. God had already been preparing Bezalel. God does not call us into things He has not already planned, prepared and equipped us to do.

The Foolish Things

The people God called were doing something much lesser than what God called them to. God found many men and women in the Bible in the midst of their own foolishness when He called them. David was taking care of his father's sheep in the middle of nowhere. No one could see him or see that God was preparing him to become the next king of Israel. The disciples were busy fishing, mending and washing nets. They failed to catch anything and had no idea they would spend the rest of their lives catching men for the Kingdom of God. The woman by the well was drawing water from the well. Elisha was busy working the plow, but left that for the prophetic call. Excuses like, "But Lord, I am not educated in this, nobody has ever done that in my family, or really, Lord, of all the people who could probably do this and do it well, You decided to pick me!?!"

Doubt often hurts us. Being rejected in the past and

failing feeds doubt and keeps us trapped in the place where we failed. The Bible is full of lives whose jaws dropped, some hid out of fear and disbelief, others bargained with God and suggested He use their siblings instead; others laughed hysterically, and some said they would only believe it after they saw the hole in his hand created by the nail and touched it. God never calls the equipped; He instead equips those that He calls. Ours is to trust Him, cooperate with Him, Believe Him, Obey Him and Follow where He leads.

God is in the habit of using nobodies. God never chose the majority of those He chose from the elite, the highly educated, and the ranks of the wise. God uses our weakness, foolishness and lowliness, so He alone can be glorified. Everything God does is according to His design and not our shortcomings. God uses anybody, regardless of education, past, wealth or vocation. By design, He used harlots, prostitutes, adulterers, a Gentile woman, children, tax collectors, drunkards, the aged, murderers, persecutors and the list goes on.

Creative Imagination

There is nothing dull or boring about God. He created three primary colors with more than 10 million different hues. We cannot even see all the colors that He made. He created texture; rhythm, movement, sound, music and seasons, and He created us out of dust, put His Spirit in us, and gave us an imagination. Imagination is probably one of our most God-like characteristics, because it is the closest we actually get to creating something out of absolutely nothing.

The imagination is like a muscle. When you use it and exercise it, it will actually work. The enemy knows this that is why he works overtime to fill our minds with inappropriate thoughts and vain imaginations. The devil is afraid of Christians because he knows too well, the authority and power we have, and the Creative birthright we inherited from God. I think this is why he uses many worldly platforms to make the average

Christian feel irrelevant and inferior. God simply wants our faith and selfless obedience, nothing else, because His strength can only be perfected in our weakness.

My thoughts started to change when I saw my thoughts mattered not just to me, but also to Eternity. The power God deposited in me has the capacity to transform the world around me. I said, "Lord, this sleeping giant needs to wake up!" It all starts with a seed planted in my mind. "The creation of a thousand forests is in one acorn." (Ralph Emerson).

Sometimes our circumstances can dominate our thoughts and this can cause a disconnect to happen from the True Vine. (John 15:5). I think it is often difficult to fathom how God can use me because of my frequent foolishness, but the confidence I have is in the finished work of Christ. Christ's sacrifice covers all my sins and failures. I have been crucified with Him, and I no longer live, but Christ is the One Who lives in and through me (Galatians 2:20). The secular world put their confidence in themselves, and in common sense, but as children of God, our confidence is deeply rooted in our faith and in Jesus Christ.

Creativity is connected to Good News

Having creativity without putting our creativity to work negates it. Our creative expression is good news for those who are lost. Creativity is connected to missions. If I have the courage to express and share the gifts God has given me, others can experience my gift. They can discover what they are good at and what to do with their lives through my obedience. Creativity is also a form of worship. We create order out of the chaos and confusion. Without our creativity, there would be no structure or order. Jesus Christ is our model for creativity. He spoke from boats, beaches, and hillsides. He multiplied fish and bread, He cursed a fig tree, and He drew in the sand. If anything, we ought to learn from His example, and carry our creative gifting into every area of ministry we function in.

In the Book of Genesis, in the account of the Garden of Eden and the creation of Adam and Eve, God gave us a mandate to do something before we got a command not to do something. When Jesus was departing to Heaven, He gave us a command to do something as well. The knowledge of the glory of God can spread throughout this entire earth through what we are willing to do. The earth should be completely covered with the glory of God through what we tell the world about Christ and the work of our hands that testify of Who He is and what He can do.

Where God Hides Ideas

"It is the glory of God to conceal a matter,
But the glory of kings is to search out a matter"
(Proverbs 25:2).

The Bible says that God hides things on purpose because He receives more glory when He conceals a thing, rather than making it obvious. Our glory is to seek out a thing and find out what God has hidden for us to find. I think God hides revelation and ideas from us, not to punish, but to protect us sometimes from failure to take hold of that responsibility. Proverbs 25:2 says that, "It's the glory of kings to search out a matter." This leads me to think that the mysteries of God are my inheritance. God hides these mysteries so we seek Him for the answers to what problems need solving in the world.

God has Hidden Things for us

Everything God created also carries a seed within itself. I often think about trees and how God spoke and trees happened. We see trees, but everyone sees something different. For some, it is the fact that trees provide shade, shelter, oxygen, food or beauty, but for others who create products we use today, they see paper, furniture, rubber, chewing gum, aspirin, acne medicine, sponges, energy, tool handles, and many other things. God said one thing and many things were hidden in that one thing. The reality of God is in everything He has made. God's glory is revealed in all of creation, and we live surrounded by His mind and His heart in the things around us. I love the fact that in everything God created He left something hidden in it for us to find.

I watched a TED Talk by Steven Berlin Johnson (2014) about the connection between science, technology and personal experience. Something jumped in my spirit as I listened. Johnson talked about the idea that our environments often lead to unusual levels of innovation. It all begins in our brains and has a pattern:

An idea – is a network of neurons firing in sync with each other inside the brain.

The question I had was, "Well, how do you get your brain into environments that fire these networks?" The Lord then took me to Proverbs 25:2, which says, "It is the glory of God to conceal a matter, but the glory of kings is to search out a matter." Johnson shared a story that blew my mind. Timothy Prestero works with Design that Matters, and he had an idea to try and help tackle infant mortality in the developing world in Africa. He and his team created a modern neonatal incubator that cost $40,000 to keep premature babies from villages in Africa warm. The incubator was sent to a village in Africa. It worked for two years, but then broke down and nobody could fix it. The villages did not have access to the spare parts.

Prestero decided to do some research and try to find an alternative. He asked himself, "What resource do developing countries have that could solve the parts problem for the incubator." Africans are pretty good about keeping their cars running, so he found a solution in the environment. He built a neonatal incubator out of automobile parts and called it the "neonurture device." It looks like an incubator on the outside, but the inside runs on car parts. Some of the best ideas we have come from our environments. It may not seem like much, but often God will take the little you have and do much with it. He did that with the little boy's five loaves and two fishes!

CHAPTER THIRTEEN
RE-ESTABLISHING OUR CREATIVE BIRTHRIGHT

"Yours, O Lord, is the greatness, The power and the glory,
The victory and the majesty;
For all that is in heaven and earth is Yours;
Yours is the kingdom, O Lord,
And You are exalted as head over all.
Both riches and honor come from You,
And You reign over all. In your hand is power and might;
In Your hand it is to make great And to give strength to all.
Now therefore, our God,
We thank You And praise Your glorious name"
(1 Chronicles 29:11-13).

I recently had been meditating and thinking about the account of Creation and the showdown that happened between Moses and Pharaoh in the Book of Exodus. I used to think the 10 plagues were a demonstration of God's power, but there is so much more to the account. I did not see that there was actually a connection between the story of Creation and the 10 plagues in the Book of Exodus. The plagues were important because of their meanings, their order and their number. I think they were creative because they went completely against nature, put the Egyptian gods in their place, and the similarities they had with the account in Genesis 1 and 2. I love how the Word of God has so many connections. This may be a little off the topic, but I was thinking about the fact that when Moses threw his staff down and it became a serpent, the last time we saw a serpent was in Genesis 3 in the Garden of Eden. Moses throwing down the staff and it turning to a serpent is a reminder to the enemy that God had cursed the serpent, and that he was to crawl on his belly and grovel in the dust as long as he was to live (Genesis 3:14).

The account of Creation in the Book of Genesis went from chaos and darkness to structure. The 10 Plague account went from structure to chaos and darkness in the land of Egypt. God has a serious conversation in the 10-plague account where Moses makes 10 statements to Pharaoh about Who God is. I wondered why it took 10 Plagues to get the message across. It may be that God is a God of order, and Pharaoh's behavior was so anti-creation and out of line that it needed to be addressed on all levels—it was violating the natural flow of what God intended in the beginning. God had to set the record straight and put Pharaoh in his place. God had to let Pharaoh know, that He controls ALL of creation, including Egypt and Pharaoh.

God showed Pharaoh Who He is by reversing what He had done in Genesis 1 and 2 in the Creation account when the 10 plagues happened. It was like God knitted a beautiful knit sweater and then unraveled it in the 10 plagues incident. Then knit it back together when He was done making His point. The same God Who is the Creator of the entire universe is capable of destroying, and we have the same capacity to create and destroy as children of God. I loved the irony of the Egyptians being engulfed in darkness in the Book of Exodus during the plague of darkness, and the Israelites were enjoying light in Exodus 10:23. This passage of scripture interestingly mirrors Genesis where God separates light from darkness.

The plagues remind us that this account was a miraculous involvement of God. The plague of frogs represents Pharaoh's pride being out of control since in those days in Egypt frogs represented fertility. The frogs ending up everywhere, including where they were naturally not supposed to be. This shows how much pride was consuming Pharaoh's heart. The fact that the sorcerer's could not reverse the water turning into blood is a reminder that the devil cannot reverse what God says. We have a covenant with God through the blood of Jesus Christ that cannot be reversed. Pharaoh's behavior and lack of reverence for God and Creation also came with dire consequences.

Isaiah 40:28 says, "Do you not know? Have you not heard? The Everlasting God, the Lord, the Creator of the ends of the earth does not become weary or tired. His understanding is inscrutable?" God is all knowing, all seeing, and all understanding. He knew exactly how to deliver the Israelites from the bondage of Egypt, and in the 10 plagues, we see that even nature is not outside of His control. When He told the Israelites to leave Egypt, He knew exactly how He would deliver them and how to deal with a stubborn pharaoh.

When God wants to take us out of ourselves, out of the past, out of limitation, out of bondage, out of everything that hinders His creative mandate for our lives, He knows exactly how to show us what it means for Him to be God.

Rekindle Creativity

Give the Holy Spirit permission to rekindle the possibilities, connection, purpose, identity, resilience, freedom, curiosity, adventure and faith you had. We are already created to be creative; sometimes, it just takes having a light bulb moment or revelation that 'as God is, so are you.' Creativity is a part of who you are, and is a gift from God. How we use it is our gift to Him. I always cringe when I start to think about how the years have started creeping up on me. I am learning to keep my creative thought process younger than my calendar age because "we are always the same age inside." (Gertrude Stein)

Sometimes, we don't step into what we were created for because we don't know we can even go there. Our creativity should come from abiding in Christ. He is our Vine and Apart

From Him, we cannot do anything. Determine to stop saying:

- it's too late
- break the compulsion to compare
- stop imagining failure
- creativity is a luxury I can't afford
- fearing people and consequences
- give yourself permission to be the person God created you to be
- stop fearing rejection
- dismissing your dreams
- waiting until you have enough money
- decide to abandon your inner critic

I decided to get past the power of the cross to the power of the resurrection. The cross happened, and it matters, but then Jesus could not stay in the tomb. There was a resurrection that took place. There is great confidence in knowing my value is not determined by the things I feel or see about God. It is in what He has already said and done. Our values also create greater value. I have often tried to achieve goals before realizing and affirming to myself that I had the identity in Christ to achieve those goals.

Before we can believe for good things to happen through us, we must believe good things about ourselves. A while ago, I had to step back and look at my life and what I was doing. Everything I was doing with my life was a reflection of the belief system I had about myself. My desire is to walk in revelation of my birthright to be creative. God forbid I ever forget who I am and whose I am in Jesus Christ.

Easy steps to getting started
1. Define your dream.

What are you passionate about? What is God saying to you? What is the one thing you would do if you had all the resources you needed?

2. Believe what God is showing you.

Make a commitment to your dream and commit it to the Lord. Ask Him to show you what steps you need to take for it to come to pass. God can give you a strategy, but you need to decide that you actually want that dream to happen.

3. Remember Fear is part of the process.

4. Take Action.

What do you need to do to get started? Go and do it—start somewhere.

5. Your Ideas Matter

Remember that your ideas matter because God loves you and trusts you enough to release them to you. He wants nothing more than to partner with you.

6. Mistakes are lessons not excuses to give up and not try again.

7. Value decisions whether they are big or small.

Every decision you make has a consequence and matters. What you do in life determines who you become.

8. Visualize and Plan

Mental preparation is important. If you have nothing in front of you, you won't do anything. You can start by making a vision board, with symbols of what God has put on your heart. Keep a vision journal close by to write in it regularly. Keep a progress section in the journal that shows what progress you have made and what goals you have accomplished. There are times you just need to go to certain places and see similar ideas to the one God has given you.

There are experiences we can have that can really inspire us if we allow ourselves to experience them. Sometimes all it takes is walking across the street to the park, or tasting a local delicacy you have never tried. We all don't have to go to Silicone Valley to see the Tech world's corporate headquarters state of the art buildings, or one of Milan's most treasured ballet venues, the Teatro alla Scala. I remember my first Disney trip to Anaheim California; I could not sleep that night because all sorts of ideas were sprouting in my mind after that experience. There is something about being in an atmosphere or experiencing a place or product that changes you and causes you to see things you had never seen before.

Know your Craft

"I fear not the man who has practiced 10,000 kicks once, but I fear the man who has practiced one kick 10,000 times"(Bruce Lee). Those are words of wisdom for mastering your craft. The best writers read a lot; they possess a keen ear for language and for words. The greatest artists and painters know their medium and see everything they create, big or small, as entirely worthy of the same attention. Focusing on our passion drives enthusiasm, and passion is connected to calling. Gifted musicians know their instruments and what sounds they want to draw out of them and when. Mastery does not demand perfection, but that you consistently do your best. Mastering anything requires tremendous sacrifice and investing time and forsaking other worthless pursuits. Creating is not convenient, but it's worth the sacrifice. "We are defined by what we make time to do, not by what we do when we have time."(Kate Matsudaira).

In building or creating with a purpose, there are seven important things to remember:

1. The vision belongs to God.
2. Prayerfully pursue the vision.
3. God qualifies you for the vision.

4. God expects you to take ownership of the vision.

5. Pursue the vision diligently, even when obstacles and hindrances come and people try to discourage you.

6. Don't be intimidated by people or the vision.

7. Be discerning about whom you tell the vision. The vision may be for an appointed time. (Habakkuk 2:3).

8. Someone will be inspired by your courage and your faith when the vision comes to fruition.

Things Worth Fighting for

Two inspiring Christians and business people from Africa are Mr. Strive and Mrs. Tsitsi Masiyiwa. The humility they have as a couple challenges me in so many ways. Mr. Strive Masiyiwa is a servant of Christ and an African multibillionaire. He and his wife, Tsitsi, over two decades ago took the Zimbabwean government to court in an intense legal battle over a dream God placed in his heart. Masiyiwa had a vision to start Zimbabwe's first mobile telecommunications company, but the Zimbabwean government wanted exclusive monopoly rights to manage and operate all telecoms in Zimbabwe. I love his story because it paints a picture of a life totally surrendered to the Lord. God has honored and favored him so much because of his faithfulness, but also because of the condition of his heart.

The high court of Zimbabwe ruled in favor of Masiyiwa, and today, Econet wireless is a thriving telecommunications company and Zimbabwe's largest mobile telecoms firm with over 6 million subscribers. The company has operations in Johannesburg, Burundi, Lesotho, Kenya, Nigeria, Botswana, and Rwanda. (Mfonobong Neshe, 2013).

I remember the first time I heard his testimony; I cried because I was so challenged by how intelligent and creative he was, and even more deeply moved by his love for the Lord and his humility. He is the richest man in Zimbabwe, but he has something bigger in his pocket and bank account than money. He has a very personal relationship with God and a big heart.

I read a few nuggets he shared in an interview with Forbes (2013) that I want to share. I felt his wisdom was so relevant to our generation and re-establishing our birthplace of creativity …

1. Pray Hard

"God will do nothing except you pray,
and you have to be clear what you want."
- Strive Masiyiwa

Judging from his success in his marriage, his children, and his business, prayer does work! The secret is to pray, even when you don't see results. Never cease to pray and to trust God. Faith is important, and you cannot please God without faith. When we, "come to God, we must believe that He is, and that He is a rewarder of those who diligently seek Him" (Hebrews 11:6).

2. Identify a Human Need and Meet it

His focus was not to wake up and make billions. He just wanted to impact lives and give as many people in Africa as possible an access to a great telecommunications experience. He wanted to solve a problem. Many times, we get caught up in trying to pay our own bills, and miss out on the fact that where we are is still an opportunity to be a blessing. "Do not withhold good from those to whom it is due, when it is in the power of your hand to do so" (Proverbs 3:27). We are created to do more than just hustle, work and pay bills. Everyone has an opportunity and a mandate to make a difference.

"If you reach out to meet the needs of the people
around you, you will wear the crown."
- Strive Masiyiwa

3. Give

What you give comes back tenfold. To date, I think he and Mrs. Masiyiwa educate more than 42,000 orphans through a scholarship fund they founded.

4. Work Hard and Stay Focused

"Lazy people are always doomed to fail."
- Strive Masiyiwa

5. Be Patient and Relentless

Don't ever give up. The government threatened him and rejected him, but God fought the battle on his behalf. He was tried and tested and went through a series of frustration and rejection, but God honored his faith.

"Success hardly occurs in a split second,
you need to learn to wait for your moment."
- Strive Masiyiwa

Cultivating Creativity

Creating and innovating comes from our habits. I think creativity has a lot to do with your attitude toward life. If you think you are creative, you will attract people, circumstances and situations in line with your thoughts. One of my goals this year is to creatively respond to every problem I encounter, whether it's big or small. Being creative should not be burdensome, but the way I decide to live. It helps to grow creativity in a soil that nourishes, encourages and rewards us through a community of people who will support and encourage us. It is also important to remember that creativity flows out of a heart that is brimming over with generosity.

I wrote down a few finale summary nuggets for what we talked about in the book. Thank you for reading it. Congratulations, you survived over 134 pages of ideas God put on my heart. I hope something blessed you, inspired you, provoked you, made you smile, and pushed you to go and do what you were created to do …

1. Don't censor or filter the ideas God releases

Everything that seems foolish can work. Some of the greatest creative ideas came out of foolishness. The Word says God uses the foolish things of this world to shame the wise.

2. Creativity comes from God

God built and wired our brains to generate creative ideas. It does help to spend time with God. I know it certainly does help me. When I made solo attempts at anything, especially when I was trying to write this book, I ended up becoming very frustrated and moved on to something else. But when I asked the Holy Spirit for help, and invited Him to help me, it made all the difference. Purpose in your heart to partner with God because you partner with the Creative Father and Friend!

3. Surround yourself with creative company

Creativity is a breeding ground for creativity. Impartation does really happen by association. There is something about being around other creative individuals that gets my creative juices flowing. I feel like I am surrounded by fountains and not by drains. (Laura Moncur). I love being around people who think differently from me, but often I have to prune and weed out relationships that do not cause me to grow or challenge me as an artist because these relationships don't inspire me. Instead, they cause me to quickly forget who I am and what my assignment is.

4. Avoid living by what others think

This is the quickest way to squash what God wants to release through us. The enemy really works overtime in attacking our thoughts because he doesn't want us to think about what God wants to do in our lives. Thinking on the things God says can catapult you into things you never even dreamed you could walk in. It gives you an added advantage.

It is important to give yourself permission to think. Doers are great thinkers. Leonardo Da Vinci was a great painter who had many critics, but he did not focus on the thoughts of others about him. He focused on the possibilities he had with expressing his craft. He was a very thoughtful artist and a meticulous scientist who mixed his paints, studied anatomy, understood how pigments can be mixed, loved science and art. His combining of science and art in his craft made him a great artist because he stretched his thinking (science) and in his doing (art). He did not just produce beautiful paints, but he went the extra mile and thoughtfully studied the entire process and subject matter, including mixing his own pigments.

5. Be inquisitive and curious

Some of our best ideas come from problems we encounter that need to be solved.

6. God has hidden things in creation for us, not from us

God is amazing! I love how we are not just surrounded by His glory, His Heart and the things He has made, but we are also surrounded by the ideas He has hidden for us to find. Many of those ideas are hidden in the things He has made. I am trying to get in the habit of asking the Holy Spirit to show me and point out things God has hidden for me to find.

7. Pull into reality what God has planted inside you

I was thinking about a plant or tree that is planted. We cannot see the seed that is deposited in the ground until that seed starts to germinate, grow, and push itself out of the soil. Sometimes we just need to push those ideas out, until others can see them. Our creative ideas can change the world and the world would be diminished without every idea God intended for us to share. We must have the personal conviction that all our creative ideas matter and can add value to the lives of those around us. Some people need to experience the ideas we have because their whole life depends on what we have been given.

8. Connect with those who have succeeded at what you are trying to do

Desire to get around the right kind of heroes, and before you know it, you will be someone's hero, too. There is a difference between our resume virtues and eulogy virtues. If asked to choose which matters to you more, the appropriate and more popular choice would be the eulogy virtues. But funny enough, those are not the ones we think about the most.

9. Have a defined target market

Let your market be the whole world, in business and in life. If you aim at nothing, you won't hit anything.

A Last Story

Potatoes, Eggs and Coffee beans

A daughter complained to her father that her life was miserable and that she had tried so many ventures that all failed. She was tired of always fighting, always struggling, always getting disappointed whenever she pursued a creative venture. It seemed when she thought she was making one step forward she would soon be taking one backward.

Her father was a chef, who pondered on what his daughter shared. One day he asked her to sit in another room while he went to the kitchen, and filled three pots with water and placed each pot over a burner on high. Once each pot began to boil, he placed a potato in the first pot, eggs in the second pot, and ground coffee beans in the third pot.

He let them boil and left them for a while, without letting his daughter in on what he was doing. The daughter wondered what on earth he was doing in the kitchen as she waited impatiently for him to give her a solution to her problem.

After 20 minutes, he turned off all the burners and took the potatoes out of the pot and placed them in a bowl. He pulled out the eggs and also placed them in a bowl.

He ladled the coffee out and placed it in a mug, added some sugar and almond and caramel flavored cream. He called his daughter into the kitchen and ask "My daughter what do you see?"

A little frustrated she said, "Potatoes, eggs and coffee!"

"Look closer," he replied, "and touch the potatoes, peel the eggs and taste the coffee."

She did what he asked, a little annoyed said, "the potatoes are soft, the eggs are boiled and the coffee brewed, what are you trying to say dad!"

He then sat her down and said "the potatoes were unrelenting and hard before they boiled but the boiling made them soft and weak.

The eggs were fragile and could easily be dropped and the shell crack and the liquid spill out, but when they boiled the inside became very hard. The ground coffee beans were different . . . when exposed to boiling water they changed and something new that tasted and smelt good was created."

"Which of the three are you?" he asked, "when things happen that test your creative ideas how do you respond? Are you like the potato that softens and withdraws, or the egg that hardens and becomes bitter and negative, or are you like the coffee beans that find new possibilities it testing situations, and turns itself into something that smells and tastes good."

We have all made mistakes in the past, and we have

often been the greatest deterrent to our own progress, but something to always remember is that you are always way ahead of those who are not trying at all. You may not be exactly where you want to be but make necessary steps to move in that direction and God will honor your faith.

A last question I had for you was . . . If today were the last day of your life here on earth, would you want to do what you are planning to do today? If the answer is no, then today is that day for everything to change. Go get 'em tiger!

Prayer

Heavenly Father, thank you for the life reading this, my precious brother or sister. I ask today that you would reach the deepest part of their heart and all the cracks, corners and crevices of their lives and do a significant and deep work that will outlast them. Thank you, Lord, that today marks a new day and an encounter and opportunity to go so much further, much deeper, much higher, much wider than they have ever gone as they relate to you the Creative and Almighty God. Thank you for giving them the grace to not be so hard on themselves and the wisdom to not sit and do nothing.

Thank you, Lord, that in this moment the scales of fear, rejection, doubt and every hindrance they can see or cannot see fall off in Jesus name. May they begin to see you in a way they have never seen you before, hear from you in ways they never imagined, and experience your overwhelming love. Give them the boldness to embrace whatever it is that you love so much about them. And remind them that the price Jesus Christ paid covered it all.

Holy Spirit, I now ask you to quicken their spirit, with deep insight, unsearchable wisdom, with ideas, revelation and dreams they never saw before. Awaken the creative giant that has always been there in Jesus mighty name! Amen.

ABOUT THE AUTHOR

Chipo Shiloh Moyo is best described as a hive of creativity. She is also a pastor, a preacher, an artist and a musician. She has studied a variety of disciplines, including a BSc in Psychology, Bachelor of Arts in Fashion and Graphic Design, Associate's in Business Administration, BSc in Communications, and an Advanced Studies Diploma in Pastoral Ministry. In 2007, she founded Shiloh Luxury Handcrafted Greeting cards, a luxury gift company that creates with purpose. She is the Founder of Girls Matter International, a global ministry that is helping restore young women in poor communities and helping them realize that they are a product of the purpose of God and not their circumstances.

Visit us at:

www.theshilohboutique.com

NOTES - BIBLIOGRAPHY

Australian Bureau of Statistics, 2011

Amanpour, Christiane. "Woman Opens Heart to Man Who Slaughtered Her Family." *CNN*, Cable News Network, 15 May 2008, www.cnn.com/2008/WORLD/africa/05/15/amanpour.rwanda/.

BBC News Video address by Malala Yousafzai, July 2013

CBS NEWS, World's wonder drug, Rome Neal, eb 10, 2004

Chironna, Mark. "Step Into the Rhythm of the Holy Spirit." *Charisma Magazine*, Charisma Magazine, 3 Mar. 2015, www.charismamag.com/site-archives/1369-slw-spiritual-growth-/worship/9422-dancing-with-god.

Christensen, Tanner. The Creativity Challenge: Design, Experiment, Test, Innovate, Build, Create, Inspire, and Unleash Your Genius. Adams Media, 2015.

Clear, James. "The Science of Positive Thinking: How Positive Thoughts Build Your Skills, Boost Your Health, and Improve Your Work." *The Huffington Post*, TheHuffingtonPost.com, 10 July 2013, www.huffingtonpost.com/james-clear/positive-thinking_b_3512202.html

Cooper-White, Macrina. "Here's Why Birds Fly In A 'V' Formation." The Huffington Post, TheHuffingtonPost.com, 16 Jan. 2014, www.huffingtonpost.com/2014/01/16/why-birds-fly-in-v-formation_n_4609100.html

Craig-Purcel, Wendy. "Ask Yourself This - Could They Be Wrong." Ask Yourself This: Questions to Open the Heart, Expand the Mind and Awaken the Soul, Unity House, 2009.

Crouse, David. "1. Soils and Plant Nutrients." NC State Extension Publications, North Carolina State University , 25 Feb. 2015, content.ces.ncsu.edu/extension-gardener-handbook/1-soils-and-plant-nutrients.https://content.ces.ncsu.edu/

extension-gardener-handbook/1-soils-and-plant-nutrients

Csikszentmihalyi, Mihaly. Creativity: Flow and the Psychology of Discovery and Invention. HarperCollins Publishers, 2013.

Csikszentmihalyi, Mihaly. Creativity: the Psychology of Discovery and Invention. Harper Perennial Modern Classics, 2015

Dahir, Abdi Latif. "Africa Has Too Few Universities for Its Fast Growing Population." Quartz Media Africa, Quartz Media, 5 Jan. 2017, qz.com/878513/university-education-is-still-a-dream-many-in-africa-are-yet-to-attain/.

Dussutour et al. Communal Nutrition in Ants. Current Biology, May 12, 2009; DOI: 10.1016/J.CUB.2009.03.015

Contributed by Stacey Freedenthal, PhD, LCSW, Self-Compassion Topic Expert Contributor. "How to Turn Self-Hatred into Self-Compassion." *GoodTherapy.org Therapy Blog*, GoodTherapy.org, 27 July 2017, www. goodtherapy.org/blog/how-to-turn-self-hatred-into-self-compassion-1112135.

Fumbi Chima, 2016 March 7, How creativity empowers women, Diplomatic courier

Fromke, Devern F. Seeing God's Widsom In His Ways. Master Press, 1995

Gavanghan, Julian. "The Bug Society: Scientists Excavate Underground Ant City That Rivals the Great Wall of China with a Labyrinth of Highways." Daily Mail Online, 2 Feb. 2012, www.dailymail.co.uk/sciencetech/article-2095335/ Underground-ant-city-Brazil-rivals-Great-Wall-China-labyrinth-highways.html

Gender equality, heritage and creativity UNESCO report, Oct 13, 2014

GLOBAL PARTNERSHIP FOR EDUCATION

Goins, Jeff. The Art of Work: a Proven Path to Discovering What You Were Meant to Do. Thomas Nelson, 2015

GSMA Intelligence digital analysts, 2017

Henley William E. in Loveman, Robert. *A Book of Verses.* J.B. Lippincott Company, 1900.

International, Inc. Advanced Solutions. "Children of Alcoholics." Children of Alcoholics, American Association for Marriage and Family Therapy , 2002, www.aamft.org/iMIS15/AAMFT/Content/consumer_updates/children_of_alcoholics.aspx.

Jakes, T. D. Soar!: Build Your Vision from the Ground Up. Faith Words Large Print, 2017

Jeschke, Melanie M. *Inklings.* Harvest House Publishers, 2004

Kelley, Tom, and David Kelley. Creative Confidence: Unleashing the Creative Potential within Us All. William Collins, 2015.

Lopes, Carlos – exec secretary – UN Economic Commission for Africa

Lydia Dishman, Fast Company, www.fastcompany.com/3006255/where-are-all-women-creative-directors, 2013.

Maathai, Wangari. "Wangari Maathai - Nobel Lecture." *Nobelprize.org*, The Nobel Foundation, 10 Dec. 2004, www.nobelprize.org/nobel_prizes/peace/laureates/2004/maathai-lecture-text.html.

McNiff, Shaun. Trust the Process: an Artist's Guide to Letting Go. Shambhala, 1998

Merelli, Annalisa. "How Melinda and Bill Gates Shared School Drop-off Duty, and Changed a Community in the Process." *Quartz*, Quartz, 24 Feb. 2016, qz.com/623219/what-you-can-learn-from-melinda-and-bill-gates-kids-drop-off-schedule/.

Miller, Claire Cain. "How Society Pays When Women's Work

Is Unpaid." *The New York Times,* The New York Times, 22 Feb. 2016, www.nytimes.com/2016/02/23/upshot/how-society-pays-when-womens-work-is-unpaid.html.

Morrison, Mary Kay. Using Humor to Maximize Living: Connecting with Humor. Rowman & Littlefield Education, 2012.

New York Film Academy, 2013

Nsehe, Mfonobong. "Five Lessons From Zimbabwe's Richest Man, Strive Masiyiwa." *Forbes,* Forbes Magazine, 24 Feb. 2013, www.forbes.com/sites/mfonobongnsehe/2013/02/24/five-lessons-from-zimbabwes-richest-man-strive-masiyiwa/#5e3a532f12b1

O'Neill, Craig. "Does a Planet Need Plate Tectonics to Develop Life?" *Phys.org - News and Articles on Science and Technology,* The Conversation US, 28 June 2016, phys.org/news/2016-06-planet-plate-tectonics-life.html.

Reynolds, Michael S. Hemingway: the Paris Years. W.W. Norton & Co., 1989.

Ryan, Dale, and Juanita Ryan. Distorted Images of God: Restoring Our Vision, 8 Studies for Individuals or Groups. IVP Connect, 2012